P9-CMP-725

# THE LIVES OF ISAAC STERN

Also by David Schoenbaum

*The Violin:*
*A Social History of the World's Most Versatile Instrument*

*The German Question and Other German Questions*
(with Elizabeth Pond)

*The United States and the State of Israel*

*Zabern 1913:*
*Consensus Politics in Imperial Germany*

*The Spiegel Affair*

*Hitler's Social Revolution:*
*Class and Status in Nazi Germany*

# THE LIVES OF ISAAC STERN

David Schoenbaum

W. W. NORTON & COMPANY
*Independent Publishers Since 1923*

Printed in the United States of America
First Edition

For information about permission to reproduce selections from this book, write to Permissions, W. W. Norton & Company, Inc., 500 Fifth Avenue, New York, NY 10110

For information about special discounts for bulk purchases, please contact W. W. Norton Special Sales at specialsales@wwnorton.com or 800-233-4830

Manufacturing by Lake Book Manufacturing
Book design by Lovedog Studio
Production manager: Julia Druskin

Library of Congress Cataloging-in-Publication Data

Names: Schoenbaum, David, author.
Title: The lives of Isaac Stern / David Schoenbaum.
Description: First edition. | New York : W. W. Norton & Company, 2020. | Includes bibliographical references and index.
Identifiers: LCCN 2019050517 | ISBN 9780393634617 (hardcover) | ISBN 9780393634624 (epub)
Subjects: LCSH: Stern, Isaac, 1920–2001. | Violinists—United States—Biography.
Classification: LCC ML418.S75 S36 2020 | DDC 787.2092 [B]—dc23
LC record available at https://lccn.loc.gov/2019050517

W. W. Norton & Company, Inc., 500 Fifth Avenue, New York, N.Y. 10110
www.wwnorton.com

W. W. Norton & Company Ltd., 15 Carlisle Street, London W1D 3BS

1 2 3 4 5 6 7 8 9 0

I hug to my heart an instrument whose incompleteness is that of the human voice . . . It has made of me a gregarious musician, finding satisfaction in the company of my fellows, than which no better fate can befall any man, who is not a born cynic, during the brief term of his terrestrial existence.

—Walter Willson Cobbett,
*Cobbett's Cyclopedic Survey of Chamber Music*,
vol. 2 (Oxford and Toronto, 1963), p. 539.

To all those living room quartet players in
Madison, Minneapolis, Bonn, Hamburg, Prague,
Jerusalem, London, St. Louis and Iowa City
who taught me that Cobbett got it right.

# Contents

# Acknowledgments

ANYONE WHO WRITES A BOOK KNOWS THAT IT TAKES A village. My village, no last-not-least about it, begins with my wife. But I also want to thank the following for their patience and expertise:

The staff of the Performing Arts Reading Room and the Music Division of the Library of Congress
The staff of the New York Public Library
The staff of the San Francisco Public Library
The staff of the Juilliard Library

And the following for crucial help with questions: Charles Beare, Jacques Boubli, James Oliver Buswell, Marta Casals Istomin, Eugene Drucker, Leon Fleisher, Gino Francesconi, John Freeman, Miriam Fried, David Fulton, Vadim Gluzman, Alon Goldstein, Robert Gottlieb, Henry Hardy, Steven Honigberg, Joseph Horowitz, Eun-Mee Jeong, John Kongsgaard, Joshua Kosman, Allan Kozinn, Jaime Laredo, Norman Lebrecht, Ruth Leon, Maria Majno, Lynne Normandia, Amit Peled, Jason Price, Sharon Robinson, Mariam C. Said, Jeffrey Scheuer,

Zina Schiff, Michael Schoenbaum, Miriam Schoenbaum, Philip Setzer, Nancy Shear, Steve Sherman, Will Shortz, Joel Smirnoff, Ivan Stefanovic, Arnold Steinhardt, David Stern, Linda Reynolds Stern, Michael Stern, Shira Stern, Jaap Van Wesel, Noah Stern Weber, James Wolfensohn.

# Preface

"A simple fact emerges for me," Robert Bein, the late Chicago violin dealer, pointed out to me some years ago. "Violins and violinists are very damned interesting."[1]

I didn't need much persuading. But I thought the elegance and economy of what he said and how he said it were worthy of a bumper sticker or T-shirt. It also puzzled me that what was so obvious to us seemed a well-kept secret to friends, family, and my historian colleagues.

As it happened, I was engaged at the time in a project intended to make his point in what became a book of something over 700 pages, backnotes and a wonderful index included.[2] Off and on, it required extended absence from home, got me to St. Petersburg, Tokyo, Shanghai, and took the better part of twenty years to write.

It was a few years more before I realized how much time and how many Canadian trees I might have spared had I only learned earlier what I now learned almost by coincidence. The first coincidence was the publication of a short biography of Barbra Streisand in an academic series on notable Jewish lives. The second was my inadvertent discovery that Isaac Stern had left 140 boxes, some 200 linear feet, of personal papers to the Library of Congress.

First, if anyone qualified as a notable Jewish life, I told myself, it was Stern. If anyone was born to show and tell what makes violins and violinists very damned interesting, it was also Stern. Second, I now lived about forty minutes from the Library, a generic commute on the Washington Metro. There they were, all under one roof: Performing Arts, Still Photos, Motion Pictures, Manuscripts, Law Library, and Current Periodicals included. It was the closest I'd ever got in fifty-two years as an archival researcher to one-stop shopping. For the next nine months the Performing Arts Reading Room would be my home away from home.

In fact, as I would soon learn, Stern had lived not one notable Jewish life. He'd lived four of them, consecutively and concurrently, as immigrant kid, world-class professional, public citizen, and go-to guy in a startling variety of ways for a startling variety of causes and people.

Material was a problem, but not because there was too little of it. On the contrary, there was more than enough. The problem, in library language, was that the papers were unprocessed, meaning that the contents of each of those 140 boxes came as a surprise. It is devoutly to be hoped that a bibliographer will one day catalogue what is potentially a major research collection. In the meanwhile, I was working, in effect, in an extraordinarily interesting landfill.

The names alone that I found there set me on my ear. But so did random items. One of my favorites was a giant desk calendar that doubled as a daily diet and calorie log. It began, of course, on January 1. The entries ended on January 2.

There were also eighteen invitations to the White House and instructions from Sir Isaiah Berlin on how to reply to a thank-you note from the Prince of Wales after a 1985 concert in London. The first option was no reply at all, which Berlin suspected would not even be noticed. The second was "the full potent manner," e.g., "It was so kind of you, Y.R.H., to have sent me so moving an acknowledgment of the service which I was deeply honoured to lay at Y.R.H.'s feet." The third possibility was "a perfectly natural note," with the option to add "if you wish to, that you much enjoyed your conversation with him after the concert, whether you did or not."

But after a dozen or so boxes, I noticed a couple of subtexts that extended through the whole collection. It's these that seem to me most interesting today in a world already quite different from the one he left in 2001.

The first was the significance of time and place. Without the talent, temperament, brains and stamina that most of us can barely imagine, Stern wouldn't have been Stern. But he also enjoyed an uncommonly, even uniquely, good time to be an American, as well as an historically good place to be a Jew.

His luck began at age ten months, when he got to the United States three years before Congress slammed the golden door on open immigration. He grew up in a city with a musical infrastructure and social support system as good as any in Europe. Why go to Europe? Europe came to him.

Even in the Depression and war years, there was an established concert circuit, network radio included. By his early twenties, he'd lucked into a relationship with Sol Hurok, a manager as talented as himself, and played the Carnegie Hall recital that got him to the major leagues.

He then lucked into full employment, postwar prosperity, the GI bill, a bumper crop of university concert series for a bumper crop of first-time college students, and even Hollywood.

Postwar superpower was another comparative advantage for American artists. Washington wanted the world to know that there was more to America than money, chewing gum and cowboy movies. Ambassadors begged Stern to visit. Foreign impresarios and summer festivals couldn't get enough of him.

Technology was a multiplier, too. Propeller-driven, then jet-propelled air travel got him in hours to places that Fritz Kreisler and Maud Powell could only reach in days. The coming of the LP record made it possible for its buyers to hear him play uninterrupted movements, even whole concertos and sonatas, in the comfort of home or dorm room.

The second subtext came to me incrementally as I continued on my way. What I was looking at, I realized, were Stern's answers to the questions attributed to Hillel in one of the most famous of all nonbiblical texts. "If I am not for myself, who will be for me? If I am only for myself, what am I? And if not now, when?"

The first question was no problem. He himself declared in his memoir that his contemporaries—Jascha Heifetz, David Oistrakh, Nathan Milstein, his protégés Itzhak Perlman and Pinchas Zukerman, and the follow-on generation, Anne-Sophie Mutter, Gidon Kremer and Midori—all played better than he did. That needn't be taken literally. When he was good, he was very,

very good. But it was true, especially as he grew older, that some nights were better than others.

He could also be self-ironic, for example about eating and talking, two of his favorite activities. First man: "I heard Isaac Stern last night." Second man: "What did he say?" He told the joke himself. From early on, self-assurance was never an issue.

The second question was no problem either. The man who saved Carnegie Hall was not a man who was in it only for himself. Nor was the man who put a newly independent, Third World Israel on the First World map, loaned instruments to needy young players and replied personally and without condescension to a fifth-grader in Oregon who wanted to know what Stern's life was like.

The third question was again no problem. With the Internet still beyond the horizon, weeks might pass before he returned to what was waiting for him in New York. But in principle, "when" almost always meant "now."

No one, including himself, claimed that he was a tzaddik, a righteous person at the highest level, let alone a Mr. Rogers. Even younger colleagues who venerated him called him a bulldozer. Norman Lebrecht, the British critic, considered him "an old fashioned *macher*,"[3] a person who knows how things get done, and gets them done. There was certainly something to this.

But he was also a great violinist, unfailingly respectful of his art and profession, good to his secretaries, attentive to his kids, loyal to his friends, supportive of the young and an exemplary citizen. Anyone still curious to know how and why violins and violinists are worth writing about need go no further than the Performing Arts Reading Room of the Library of Congress and start with Box 1.

# THE LIVES OF ISAAC STERN

I

# IMMIGRANT

*I led a double life, in public and private*
*I wanna lead it again, I'm not gonna deny it*
*I'm just like you, it's true, you know*
*Ask yourself: are you ready to go?*
*You want a double lifetime.*

"Double Lifetime,"
Loudon Wainwright III

OVER A LONG AND ACTIVE CAREER IN AN ERA STILL untouched by social media and the smartphone, the violinist Isaac Stern filled at least three Rolodexes, one color-coded, and an address book he carried on his person. There were also separate books for London, Paris and Israel. Like the 2,065 entries in Don Giovanni's catalogue, the entries in his address books could be of any age, shape or social status.

As early as 1952, celebrated composition teacher Nadia Boulanger and the Israel Philharmonic knew where to turn for help when the violinist Jean Pasquier fell and smashed his instrument, and the orchestra needed a vacuum cleaner for its guest house.[1] A fan letter from an admirer in Switzerland, addressed to Mr. Isaac Stern, The Violinist, New York, USA, arrived with no apparent problem. So did another, in Italian, from a Taiwanese soprano in Texas, addressed to Dear Dr. Violinist Isaac Stern, by Teather Opera-Metropoolitan, Manhatan Zone, New York City, Unite State of America [*sic*].

A few decades and a few lives later, the Lotos Club, a New York literary society whose membership dated back to Mark Twain, Gilbert and Sullivan, and Andrew Carnegie, was happy to co-opt Stern as a member. So was Washington's Alfalfa Club, host to an annual four-hour dinner for presidents and aspiring presidents with music by the U.S. Marine Band. At Bohemian Grove, a summer camp for "the most interesting people in the world," as one enthusiast described it, he shared a tent with Secretary of State James Baker.[2]

Before and since, there has never been a career quite like Stern's. Joseph Joachim's is the closest match. Like Stern, Joachim was an upward mobility kid from an unassuming Jewish family, who made it in the big city and the world. Born in 1831 on the Hungarian side of the Austro-Hungarian border, he grew up to be dedicatee of the Brahms and Dvořák concertos and founder of the Berlin conservatory.

His annual quartet series was not only a musical, but a civic and social, occasion. Season tickets, like furniture, were passed on like heirlooms. Facebook friends, had they existed, might have included Field Marshal Helmuth von Moltke, the hero of the Franco-Prussian War; Max Planck, the Nobel Prize physicist; and Arthur James Balfour, the British prime minister and foreign secretary. In 1907, five wagons of floral tributes and carriages as far as the eye could see escorted him to the cemetery. Like Stern's, Joachim's death qualified as news fit to print in the *New York Times*. It even qualified for an editorial.

But none connected as widely, regularly, and easily as Stern with the great, the good and not so good, the rich, powerful, famous and just folks, over years, decades and every continent but Antarctica. Among the papers at the Library of Congress are eighteen invitations to the White House, extending from the Kennedy years to the Clinton Administration.

There are also exchanges with Jack Benny, the iconic comedian; Gregory Peck, the polestar of his Hollywood generation; Maya Plisetskaya, who was to the ballet what Stern was to the violin; with Abe Saperstein of the Harlem Globetrotters and Sir Isaiah Berlin of "The Hedgehog and the Fox"; with Henry Kissinger, the Harvard conservative turned secretary of state; as well as Daniel Patrick Moynihan, the Harvard liberal turned Democratic senator from New York; with Edward Said, the prophet of Palestinian nationalism as well as Golda Meir, the pioneer Zionist, who had once denied that Palestinians existed.

There is a spontaneously jolly performance of "Auld Lang Syne" on NBC's *Today* show with William F. Buckley, whose politics could not have been more distant from Stern's if they had been Aaron Burr and Alexander Hamilton.[3] There is a faux solemn exchange in Buckley's *National Review* with Robert Bork, the conservative jurist whose Supreme Court nomination was shot down by Senate liberals, on how to make the perfect martini.[4]

Fellow San Franciscans Tony Bennett and Joe DiMaggio are represented too. But there are also congratulations from "one violinist to another" for Leo Kucinski on his retirement after fifty-two years as conductor of the Sioux City Symphony, and five grandfatherly paragraphs for an eight-year-old in Georgia, who inherited his quarter-size violin from his brother, wondered whether Stern knew "the song 'Humeresque' [*sic*]" that he'd tried with mixed success to play himself, and signed F.V. (for Future Violinist).

Anniversary calls to friends, wherever they could be reached by phone, were an endearing habit. Philip Setzer of the Emerson Quartet remembered how Stern called to play "Happy Birthday" on one of his two Guarneri del Gesù's while Setzer was having dinner with friends and colleagues at Chez André in Paris. A grateful doctor in Seattle got the instrument wrong, but not the gesture. "The greatest moment at our fiftieth wedding anniversary occurred when the telephone rang and you played a serenade to Thelma on your Stradivarius," he reported. The governor, the president of the university, and a U.S. senator had even been witnesses, he added.

"He remembered his friends," was an easily imaginable epitaph. So was "He answered his mail," though it often took him a few weeks to get to it.

We can only regret that he didn't cross lives with Loudon Wainwright III, the song writer, folk singer, humorist and actor. For anyone who knew either, it could not only be reasonably assumed that they would find plenty to talk about. They might also have fantasized about how Woody Allen or Nichols and May might turn their conversation into a movie scene.

As a man whose aptitude for life was matched only by his appetite for it, Stern would most probably have gone straight to the point. Why only two lives, he would have asked. He himself not only favored at least four. He also managed to live them, not even counting a family and private life that included three marriages and as many children.

Public and private, each life for the most part followed from the preceding one. But in many ways, as one life spilled into another in a daily cascade of mail, phone calls, appeals, reminders, meetings, memos, committee reports, interviews, rehearsals and social engagements, they were concurrent as well as consecutive.

A representative to-do list for a couple of weeks in 1988 could be extended in principle at least as far back as the 1960s and as far into the future as 2001, the year he died. There was a call from Leonard Bernstein's office about a letter expressing concern for Israeli unconcern for U.S. peace proposals. There was another from Charlotte Gilbert, director of the visitors center at the New York Stock Exchange, who wanted to talk about a visit.

Agnes de Mille, the dancer and choreographer, hoped Stern could attend her next premiere. Kay Unger of the Jerusalem Foundation wanted him at a birthday tribute for Teddy Kollek, Jerusalem's redoubtable mayor. The Lotos Club hoped he would help celebrate the fiftieth birthday of Maxim Shostakovich, the composer's son. Someone connected to cellist Gregor Piatigorsky, possibly the pianist Irina Nuzova, thanked him for arranging an appointment with Oscar de la Renta, the fashion designer. Étienne Vatelot, the violin dealer, called from Paris to chat. Galina Vishnevskaya, the wife of Mstislav Rostropovich, called from Paris to request phone numbers where Stern could be reached in Minneapolis and Detroit. Frank Hodsoll, chairman of the National Endowment for the Arts, wanted Stern in Washington for a press conference on Capitol Hill.

Visiting interviewers were regularly surprised to find him simultaneously practicing, taking phone calls and watching a ballgame on TV, admittedly with the sound off. Friends, colleagues and the secretarial staff were used to it. He'd fended off some twenty wannabe biographers over the years, he explained to an audience at Washington's Temple Sinai, where Politics and Prose, Washington's signature bookstore, had brought him to promote his newly published memoir. He had nothing to say, he told them, and still had too much to do. In part, it was his way of saying no, his version of Penelope's knitting. But it was not entirely disingenuous. Little in his schedule, calendar or temperament suggested that he spent a lot of time looking in the rear-view mirror. He was too busy living.

"Have already refused 20–30 ghosting requests," he scrawled in a note to his secretary in 1990 on how to reply to the latest inquiry. "Will first have to start taping thoughts at random."[5] But another decade would pass and he was approaching eighty before he allowed Robert Gottlieb, New York's most celebrated literary editor, to connect him with the novelist Chaim Potok. The product, a collaborative memoir stitched together from hours of taped interviews, inevitably caused him to remember a lot of people and incidents long forgotten, he told a questioner who was curious about the experience. It also caused him to reflect on things he might have done differently or better.

In 1981, Nathan Pritikin, a pioneer nutritionist with a particular interest in cardiovascular health, diabetics and weight control, advised Stern with exemplary tact that his "continuing health . . . is of supreme importance to millions of music lovers" and invited him for a twenty-six-day stay at his Longevity Center in Santa Monica. If only he could work it into his schedule, Stern replied. But he would try to work in a visit the next time he appeared at the Hollywood Bowl.

In a 1985 New Year's greeting, another fan, this time a doctor in San Angelo, Texas, sounded the same trumpet. Free medical advice was not always welcome, the doctor noted preemptively. But Stern needed to lose more weight. He preferred to see Stern on TV and hear his records at ninety than gone and forgotten at sixty-five, the doctor said. A homespun Gilbert with no apparent need of a Sullivan, he even attached a patter song.

*Now if it is your wasteline that you wish to confine,*
*Check your calories, which should be reduced down the line,*

And on it went before tailing off in a firm recommendation to lay off alcohol and tobacco and add a brisk daily walk. Stern thanked him through his secretary for the verse as well as advice he intended to take seriously, and continued to enjoy his wines and cigars.

In 1987, Alexander Schneider, his senior by twelve years and a friend since Stern was a teenager, tried to slow him down. "The most important thing is your health and I really hope you won't start your usual specialitet *mishugasses*, running for what?" he urged in the inspired linguistic bouillabaisse he served with the same gusto that Stern brought to multitasking. "You have enough *kopeken* to stop, enjoy life and play only *good* music," he added. "Let all the *chuzpenikes* run and make $ playing all the time fff or pppp and lots of *vibratissimo*."

"The conductor George Szell once told me that if I hadn't spent so much time doing other things and had just practiced more, I could have been the greatest violinist in the world," Stern acknowledged in his memoir.[6] But if he'd limited his life to music and performance, the next concert, the next tour, he added, "I would sooner or later climb the walls."

"He lived like he was immortal," a grandson recalled. "He didn't quite follow conventions or normal practices, and I think the idea of an autobiography/memoir suggested the idea that his life was coming to an end."[7]

In fact, it was. His passing, after a last and strenuous appearance in Japan and his second major heart surgery in a year, was again news fit to print far beyond the *New York Times*. Those his sun had shone upon, and there were many, those on whom it had not, and wanted it known, volley'd and thunder'd during and after his life about his art and character. But no one questioned that he'd come a long way and covered a lot of ground in his eighty-one years. No one questioned either that his story was emblematic of what Henry Luce had declared the "American Century" as far back as 1941.

Like countless American stories, this story began with immigration. Like countless Jewish stories, it also began in Eastern Europe. Known after World War I by its Polish name, Kreminiecz was a border town at the junction of Poland, Russia, Ukraine and Belarus. But its historical names alone—Bulgarian, Czech, Slovak, Macedonian, Serbian, German, Russian, Polish, Ukrainian—testified to an eventful history. In the thirteenth century, it flourished briefly as a commercial center with resident populations of Germans, Poles, Armenians and Jews, imported for their artisanal skills and merchant connections. But one thing led to another, including Mongols, Lithuanians, Poles and Cossacks. Between the sixteenth and eighteenth century, Kremenets was known as an art and publishing center. Then came the partition of Poland and the Russians, and so it remained till World War I again reshuffled the cards. In 1919 the Paris peacemakers agreed to reestablish Poland, with Kreminiecz as part of the package. But especially for Jews, the reestablishment of Poland did not mean the coming of peace.

A documented presence since the fifteenth century, the Jews of Kreminiecz had known good days and bad. In 1522, 240 Jews constituted some 10 percent of the population. After World War I, some 6,500 constituted about a third. The sixteenth century was prosperous, the seventeenth a disaster as Cossacks rebelled against Polish rule, followed by the Russian-Swedish wars against Poland-Lithuania that left a trail of collateral damage.

A diminished community recovered, found a niche in cobbling, carpentry and papermaking, grew accustomed to living in Russia and even discovered the so-called Jewish Enlightenment. Again in Poland as Russia imploded in revolution and civil war, they now found themselves the target of Ukrainian pogroms and a reconstituted Poland's systemic anti-Semitism. In the years that followed, an estimated 80,000 from the general area took off for Canada, Latin America and the United States.

Among them were Solomon Stern, about thirty, his wife Clara, née Jaffe, twenty-three, and the infant Isaac, just approaching his tenth month. The family was already well on the way to the modern world. Russian in culture, and a representative of the intelligentsia by the modest standards of Kreminiecz, his father was a dashing young man and aspiring artist, who posed for a photo in high boots and an open silk shirt with a little beard, a paintbrush and an easel. His mother had studied singing on a conservatory scholarship in St. Petersburg.

Fifty years later, when Hollywood turned to Sholom Aleichem, their son was the inevitable candidate to fiddle on the cinematic roof. But the Sterns were as remote from shtetl life as most of the movie's audience. While details were fuzzy, Stern inferred in conversation with Potok that the family had somehow left via Siberia, and made their way to San Francisco, where his mother had an elder brother. At least notionally, the New Colossus, who lifted her lamp beside the Golden Door in the harbor of New York, also lifted her lamp beside San Francisco's Golden Gate. It was now 1921, the year Buddy DeSylva and Joseph Meyer introduced "California, Here I Come" in a Broadway musical that starred Al Jolson. Three years later, Jolson would record it, unforgettably, for Brunswick. The California to which the Sterns were coming could hardly be less like the tortured and tangled world they were coming from. But California, here they came.

The immigrant experience would remain a source of pride, even a cornerstone of his identity all his life. While on tour in 1973, he fired off a fan letter to Alistair Cooke, host of *America, a Personal History*, a thirteen-part BBC series on the evolution of the United States, melting pot and huddled masses naturally included. The salutation, "Dear Mr. Cooke," was incidentally a rare indication that the addressee was one of the few somebodies that Stern, who seemed to know everybody, didn't know.

"I was with friends in a New Haven hotel room . . . , preparing to go to one of the inevitable after-concert parties," he wrote. "We were all so taken that we stayed for the entire hour, letting the hosts wait, but happy for having seen something quite special."[8]

In 1996, Stern, the fan, even found occasion to support recent newcomers actively. Upset by recent laws restricting public assistance to legal immigrants and blocking school and hospital access to undocumented immigrant children, New York's Mayor Rudolph Giuliani recruited twenty-five role models for a media event on Ellis Island, where the mayor would present them as his Immigrant Coalition in a campaign to "educate Congress and the President." As might be expected, Stern accepted the invitation, as did his protégés Itzhak Perlman, Yo-Yo Ma, Zubin Mehta and Cho-Liang Lin.

It took years to confirm how often fortune led him to the right place at the right time. But the very date of his arrival in San Francisco was already a major stroke of luck.

It was true as Malcolm Muggeridge, the veteran British America-watcher, observed in a BBC series in the early 1960s, that Europe's poor made America rich. The history of immigration to America was nonetheless a history of hot and cold. In 1830, under 2 percent of the U.S. population was foreign-born; in 1850, almost 10 percent. Between 1850 and 1930, some 5 million Germans had entered the United States; between 1820 and 1930, an estimated 4.5 million Irish and 3.5 million British. Between 1820 and 1880, the Jewish population had grown from 3,000 to 300,000, mostly immigrants from Central Europe. Between 1881 and 1924 they were followed by an estimated 2.5 million from Eastern Europe.

The Sterns were already in luck that they weren't Chinese. Immigration from China had been severely limited since 1879. In 1921 the Open Door began to close on Europeans too. The Emergency Quota Act aka the Emergency Immigration Act, though intended to be temporary, established limits that would survive until 1965. The fallout from demobilization after World War I and an economic slump at home were bad enough. They were made only the more alarming by the demographic consequences of the war, the collapse of the Ottoman and Habsburg empires, and the revolutions in Russia. There was no recorded vote on the bill in the House. But 90 of 96 U.S. senators voted to limit new immigration from any country to 3 percent of the number from that country already resident in the United States as per the 1910 census. The formula was not good news for Jews from Eastern Europe. From 1920 to 1921–22, immigration fell from a little over 800,000 to a little over 300,000.

In 1924, a still bigger hammer fell. The Johnson-Reed Act, otherwise known as the National Origins Act, reduced the 3 percent cap to 2 percent as measured by the 1890 census. This time immigration fell from a little less than 360,000 to about 165,000. But while immigration from Britain and Ireland fell by 19 percent, immigration from Italy fell by 90 percent. The metric was applicable in principle to anyplace in southern and eastern Europe. But by this time, the Sterns were safely relocated in walking distance of the Golden Gate in a city practically customized to identify and develop the musical, intellectual, even civic, potential of what was now their four-year-old.

Their destination was a second stroke of luck. San Francisco was not America's oldest or its biggest city. But by any measure, it was among America's most interesting.

The city the Sterns found on arrival was home to about half a million, almost entirely white, about a quarter foreign-born, with a little more than half included in the workforce. Trade and transport constituted roughly half the economy of what a local paper called "The Wall Street of the West."

From banker to filing clerk, a white-collar population of over 8 percent was more prominent than in other cities of similar size and larger. But seamen, longshoremen, teamsters and the building trades were well represented too. As anywhere else in urban America, ethnicity, class, occupation and neighborhood were the building blocks of politics and labor relations. The business establishment pushed back with a so-called American plan for apprenticeships, the open shop and a wage board.

With episodes of corruption and what was known as "honest graft" alternating in rondo form with episodes of reform and what was known as Good Government, politics differed little from other cities of the era. As the city emerged from the rubble of the 1906 earthquake, substantial beautification and civic improvement programs coexisted with serious labor violence.

In 1926, with much of America surfing a wave of postwar posterity, the carpenters struck and this too turned violent. Stern's father, who had left painting canvases in Russia for painting houses in San Francisco, might at least have been inconvenienced, if not directly affected. But nothing in Stern's memoir or papers suggests a six-year-old's awareness of it.

In 1934, in a very different macroeconomic landscape, the waterfront erupted. Seriously disaffected from a company union imposed on them after World War I, longshoremen demanded a closed shop, a coastwide contract from Oakland to Seattle, and a union hiring hall. Management hired strike breakers, violence again broke out, the police intervened in force and picketers were shot.

There were arrests, beatings and deportations. But there were also concessions and partial victories on contentious issues of hiring, wages and hours.

To Solomon Stern, much of this must have looked familiar. Anyone like himself, born in Russia around 1890, had residual memories of 1905 and personal experience of 1917. For millions of Americans like his son, who came of age in the 1930s, the Depression was a formative experience, for many more traumatic than World War II. Survivors, who graduated from school or college into a world of 25 percent unemployment, talked about it all their lives.

Stern, age fourteen and on the threshold of awareness, did not. Famously voluble, unfailingly articulate and frequently eloquent, he could talk well, knowledgeably and at length about virtually any subject that held his attention, be it for better or worse. But, to go by his papers and memoir, the labor wars of the early thirties were clearly not one of them. Though without explanation of where and why, he recalled how the family had moved frequently even before the Depression. He remembered how his father had sold coffee door-to-door. When money was scarce, he told Potok, the family lived on what happened to show up in the unlabeled cans that were the contemporary version of food stamps. That was it.

Or was it? A stroll through a sequence of city directories by John Freeman, a native of the city's Richmond District, who identifies himself as "shack carpenter and historian," both connects and adds some dots. First spotted in 1923, the family was settled in a mixed neighborhood close to Mt. Zion, the city's Jewish hospital. The Orthodox neighborhood, which was as close as San Francisco came to New York's Lower East Side, was eight to ten blocks to the west. It was also home to the Menuhins, whose prodigious son Yehudi, Stern's senior by four years, remained a lifelong colleague. But it was not where the Sterns lived.

Mixed neighborhoods remained the common denominator of all further moves. Most of them were in the Richmond District, a working-class neighborhood near Golden Gate Park, where a third of the city's Jews were located by the late 1930s, and such Jews as the family was likely to encounter had left traditional Orthodoxy behind. Meanwhile, his father seems to have coped in a fragile job market by changing occupations as regularly as the family changed addresses. Originally listed as a painter, he was listed as a salesman in 1936, a chauffeur in 1937, a carpenter in 1939, an artist in 1942.

Freeman, with his sociologist's eye for neighborhood comings and goings, speculates plausibly that the family's choice of addresses had something to do with the Jewish patrons who were Isaac's support group and a third stroke of luck. The connection was geometrically simple, the straight line that is the shortest distance between two points. San Francisco Jews were Stern's—and Menuhin's, and their contemporary Miriam Solovieff's, and the pianist Leon Fleisher's—good fortune because San Francisco was their good fortune.

Their story was about as old as the city. In 1848, James W. Marshall of Coloma, California, discovered gold, and thousands of Central European, predominantly German, Jews discovered America. Tens of thousands from everywhere headed west. Thousands of Jews joined and followed them. What they found might not have been the promised land. But it was certainly a land of promise.

In New York, Boston, Philadelphia or Baltimore, the established cities of the east, Jews were outsiders, late arrivals at other people's party. Here, where Demand was practically limitless and virtually everyone began as an outsider, Supply offered Jews a chance to become insiders from the start. By 1870, they constituted 10 percent of the population, more Jews than anywhere but New York. In 1895, the city elected its first Jewish mayor.

In an era of genteel anti-Semitism extending at least to the 1940s, Jews were conspicuously scarce, if not altogether absent, from the Pacific Union Club. As late as 2004, Jews seemed equally absent from the San Francisco Golf Club, whose well-tended fairways were so exclusive that even members had a hard time finding them. But well before the twentieth century, Jews were prominent in business as bankers, underwriters, real estate developers, engineers and manufacturers; in civic life as lawyers, judges, members of the chamber of commerce, board of education, civil service commission, and even in the legislature, philanthropy and cultural affairs.

As everywhere, the community also looked after its own,

beginning as might be expected with religious institutions. Founded as an Orthodox congregation in 1853 by predominantly German Jews, Temple Emanu-El had switched to Reform, complete with German-language sermons, by 1860. Six years later, the congregation moved into a new, second home. With 1,300 seats and 175-foot towers, it was as emblematic of Jewish success as the Neue Synagoge in the Oranienburger Strasse in Berlin or the Dohány Street Synagogue in Budapest that were its contemporaries.

In 1927, the congregation moved to a third home. This time the style was Levantine, with a Roman-Byzantine patio, a marble fountain, a 150-foot dome and 1,700 seats. Like any Reform synagogue of its era, it included a choir and organ. There were also 30 classrooms, including one or more where the young Isaac Stern, by his own account, became the best Hebrew reader in his Sunday School class without understanding a word of what he read. Decades later, when his grandson became a bar mitzah and he was called to the altar to recite the blessing over the Torah, he relied on a pony prepared for him by his daughter. Herself a Reform rabbi, she not only wrote out the notes of the trope for him, but also transliterated the text in Roman letters.

With all regard for the architecture, it was Emanu-El's charismatic cantor who made the connection memorable. Born in Galicia in 1887, Reuben Rinder came to America at thirteen and studied at the Neighborhood Music School (now the Manhattan School of Music). He also studied cantorial singing, most likely at the Jewish Theological Seminary. He arrived in San Francisco in 1913.

Long before his death in 1966, he had become a local institution, so respected and beloved that a Reform congregation was even prepared to overlook his Polish origins and Zionist sympathies despite serious reservations about both. Over half a century, he would commission scores from Ernest Bloch, Darius Milhaud and Paul Ben-Haim; bring Bloch to San Francisco as director of the city's young conservatory; conduct Arthur Honegger's *King David*, Handel's *Judas Maccabaeus* and *Israel in Egypt*; raise funds for Bronislaw Huberman's Palestine Symphony Orchestra; outlast five rabbis and scout talent.

In 1958, Rinder's last year of active service before seven more years of active retirement, the directors of the synagogue organized a festival of sacred music in his honor. With support from San Francisco Symphony players, the University of California chorus joined the synagogue choir in pieces by Bloch, Milhaud and others that Rinder had presumably commissioned. "Among the distinguished guests who will honor the occasion with their presence will be the famous violin virtuoso, Isaac Stern," the invitation noted.

As he told Potok, Stern himself was uncertain how he came to be enrolled at Emanu-El. It was easy to understand why he was puzzled. Reform was a mid-nineteenth-century creation, developed by and for a pioneer generation of emancipated German Jews, heavily influenced by the Lutheran practice that surrounded them. In America as in Germany, it appealed to Jews who made good in business or the professions, wore a tie, sent their kids to college, and regarded their Yiddish-speaking coreligionists from the East with a mixture of paternalism and condescension. The Sterns were already a generation away from the world of *Fiddler on the Roof.* Another generation on, Solomon Stern's granddaughter Shira would both marry and become a Reform rabbi. But the Sterns of San Francisco, while hardly Sholom Aleichem material, were hardly conventional material for Reform either.

Though Isaac was approaching thirteen and Reform offered the option, becoming a bar mitzvah did not explain the Emanu-El connection. Stern assumed that his father too was not a bar mitzvah. The family culture was Russian, not Jewish. His second language, as native speakers confirmed, was fluent faulty Russian. His third language, apparently acquired from a tutor, whose son, Pierre Salinger, would be President John F. Kennedy's press secretary, was French. Like Friday night candles, Yiddish too was unknown, although his parents understood it. "To have had a religious funeral service and to have him buried in a Jewish cemetery would have been contrary to what went on in our house," he recalled of his father's death in 1946.[9] In the end, like his father, Stern too was buried in a nonsectarian cemetery.

Though it was barely implied in Stern's interviews with Potok, the second and next Golden Gate was easy to spot. Where there was Reform, there were German Jews. Where there were German Jews, there was music. In most ways, a Stern/Emanu-El connection was as counterintuitive as a Lutheran pope. But in this case it came as easily as the ferry connection across the bay to Marin County.

It was 1911 before San Francisco had a permanent orchestra and the 1920s before there was a resident opera company. But both opera and orchestra concerts went back to the 1850s. Pillars of Emanu-El like Levi Strauss and his nephews were pillars alike of the synagogue and the symphony. Local musicians were unionized by 1869. In 1902, the union's president, Eugene (aka Handsome Gene) Schmitz, a violinist in the pit orchestra at the Columbia Theatre, was even elected mayor.

By this time the city was a well-established station on the international concert circuit. Adelina Patti, the singer, showed up in 1884; Ignaz Paderewski, the pianist, in 1896; Enrico Caruso, the legendary tenor, in 1905; the Metropolitan Opera in time for the earthquake a year later. By the time the Sterns settled in, the orchestra had engaged Yehudi Menuhin, ten, as a soloist, and Bruno Walter conducted spring and summer festivals and series. In 1924, on the threshold of electrical recording, the orchestra signed a contract with the Victor Talking Machine Company. Two years later it signed with Standard Oil for Sunday afternoon broadcasts that would continue for thirty years.

Meanwhile, a local music school took shape, launched in 1917 "with three pianos, four studios, two blackboards and 40 students," by three young piano teachers in the parental home of one of them. Violin and cello followed three years later. In 1923, the piano school incorporated as a conservatory. In 1925, it hired Bloch, whose international visibility put it on the map. Five years later, he left as things began to fall apart and the center did not hold.

The stock market crash that followed meant heavy going for the orchestra, the conservatory, and musicians in general, as well as San Francisco and the world more broadly. The coming of talkies, conventionally dated from release of *The Jazz Singer* in 1927, did not make things easier. By 1933, theater musicians, who had collectively earned $1.5 million in 1928, were down to $250,000, and 40 percent of the union's 2,500 members were unemployed. Also in the ascendant, radio picked up some of the slack. So did Hollywood. But where Hollywood meant offers San Francisco players couldn't refuse, individual gain meant institutional loss. By 1934–35, an orchestra that had already approached bankruptcy in 1926, was again looking into the abyss till a player-initiated SOS—Save Our Symphony—committee rode to the rescue. Reminding any audience that would listen that the orchestra was not only a cultural but a business asset, they lobbied tirelessly in hotels, department stores, lunch clubs, and churches. Their campaign was such a success that a referendum in support of the orchestra carried by 64 percent.

A year later the orchestra hired Pierre Monteux, an acknowledged international all-star, who had conducted—or famously tried to conduct—the legendary premiere of Igor Stravinsky's *Rite of Spring* in 1913. He stayed for seventeen years.

It was a scene that Stern knew close-up and firsthand. But once again, to go by what he recalled on the record, years that were remembered by millions of others as a decade of stress and anxiety were the years of a somewhat eccentric but essentially happy childhood.

Music was already part of it. His mother sang. His father played the piano, a clue that incidentally allowed him to infer that the family must have owned one. There were concerts. There were also records and a wind-up Victrola, though its styluses had to be replaced after five playings.

At six he was packed off for the piano lessons that were quasi-obligatory for every middle-class or aspiring middle-class child. Two years later, his decision to switch to the violin coincided with an eruption of local talent that promised to turn the "Paris of the West" and "Wall Street of the West" into the "Odessa of the West."

Born in 1916, Yehudi Menuhin, San Francisco's first prodigy, was barely out of diapers when he fell for the violin as others fall in love. His example made history. Born two years later, Ruggiero Ricci, the city's second prodigy, came to the violin, as he explained to an interviewer decades later, because his father read about Menuhin in the newspaper. It was easy to see Stern, born 1920, as another product of love, or at least of money. But it was also wrong. "I've said this in 127,862 interviews, that I didn't come home from a concert and cry for a violin," he told Potok. Coincidence really was coincidental. He took it up because a friend across the street took it up first. The friend went on to sell insurance. Stern himself went on to an education and career eccentric enough at the time, and scarcely imaginable today.

It was clear from the mountaintop that the narrative he'd walked into at age eight was specific to time and place. "The whole Jewish thing was part of the breakout from the ghetto," he told Potok, though this was unlikely to come to Potok as news. Countless young Asian children were acting out now the narrative that he did then.

But eight-year-olds are not historians. Instead, Stern absorbed the here and now of a regional cultural center with theaters in the middle of downtown, an opera house, the Veterans Auditorium where he would play his first recital, and a huge, good public library. The long view meant Oakland and Marin County, still accessible only by ferry.

A normal American kid with normal American tastes, he attended football games and memorized batting averages. He frequented a café owned by Lefty O'Doul, another San Francisco native, manager of the Triple-A Seals and a celebrated hitting instructor, whose relationship to Joe DiMaggio rather resembled his own relationship to Naoum Blinder, concertmaster of the San Francisco Symphony.

He remembered cowboy movies, whose appeal baffled his immigrant father as they baffled thousands of other immigrant fathers. There were family picnics in Golden Gate Park. There were shared watermelons, and milkshakes that needed to be eaten with a spoon. There was tennis on public courts with Nathan Ross né Rothstein, another Blinder protégé, who would make good as a Hollywood studio player. There was the world's biggest Chinatown this side of China, "with good food to match."

His mother took a serious interest in food, he told Potok, "preparing it, serving it and eating it." Food would be a recurring motif, an interest he inherited and shared, over the rest of his life. "My mother wondered why I wasn't losing weight," he added.

He read too. In 1962, he drew a blank when quizzed on his childhood preferences by Dorothy Gordon, moderator of the *New York Times*'s Youth Forums. But if something occurred to him, he would get back to her in a few months, he assured her. In fact, it was nearly forty years before the answer came to him in conversation with Potok. Interestingly idiosyncratic, it was worth the wait.

Favorite writers, possibly assigned by a tutor, included Arthur Conan Doyle, Agatha Christie, Joseph Conrad and John Dos Passos. There was also *Man, The Unknown*, by the now almost totally forgotten Alexis Carrel, a French physician and dedicated eugenicist in search of human perfection, whose pioneer vascular surgery won him a Nobel Prize in 1912. A global best-seller, published in 1935, his book was translated into nineteen languages. "It made me aware of the awesome power of the human mind," Stern recalled in his memoir. It seems unlikely that he ever touched it again.

There was only one obvious omission in what he otherwise recalled as a world of almost Norman Rockwell normality. "What did you do for school?" Potok asked. "I never went to school," Stern replied. "I'm a born illiterate," he added. The illiteracy part was meant and understood as fun. But the school part was true enough.

That Menuhin and Ricci had been eccentrically schooled was easy to explain. By the time most other kids reached school, both were already on tour and incidentally supporting their families in no apparent conflict with child labor laws. How Stern and his contemporary, Leon Fleisher, the pianist and still another local prodigy, could be school dropouts while living at home took some explaining. Officially, school attendance had been mandatory in California since 1874, when Republicans favored it, though many Democrats did not. By the dawn of the new century, Protestant and Jewish social reformers were more convinced than ever that all kids, and especially slum kids, should go to school. But in San Francisco, as in many cities, enforcement was less than zealous and universal attendance more often understood as an expression of good intentions.

By 1924, Stern was approaching school age. State law specified that "all children between the ages of eight and sixteen years, not exempted, shall attend the full time day schools for the full time the public schools of the district are in session." But it allowed for plenty of exemptions. Among them were health, physical distance from the nearest school and enrollment in a private school. As though custom-tailored for kids like Stern and Fleisher, it also allowed for at least 160 days of home schooling with a private tutor at least three hours daily between 8 A.M. and 4 P.M.

Even with cues from Potok, Stern was hard put to reconstruct what led to what after nearly seventy years. But he remembered quite clearly that he'd been taken out of school at eight, when it was decided that it was more important that he practice the violin than go to school. Unspecified connections led to the conservatory he assumed his parents had learned of from friends. His teachers there, including Robert Pollak and Nathan Abas, both immigrants like himself, brought thoroughly respectable professional credentials. But none was memorable. On the contrary, as he told Potok, "each of them found that I was progressing beyond their capacity to teach me, at a faster rate than they could handle." He recalled himself in short pants as concertmaster of the school orchestra. He also remembered playing for Bloch.

A 1986 Bloomingdale's ad shows a chubby Stern, age seven, artfully posed next to an upright piano. "Mom," he asks on a tear sheet, "do you really think that if I practice very hard, I can really get to Carnegie?"[10] His parents were supportive, even enthusiastic. But it was a question neither he nor his parents were likely to have asked in 1927. A follow-up ad a year later shows Stern, now age eight, in his first suit with long pants. "Look at the shoes," he wrote on a second tear sheet. "The suit was shinier than the shoes." He played stickball as well as recitals in them, he noted. They could well have been the only pair he owned. His mother, like countless mothers, did her bit to keep his mind on practice. But it was not long before he realized that he really wanted to practice, and the world began to take notice.

What happened next can be inferred from the reminiscence of a San Francisco contemporary some sixty-five years later. A retired doctor, still living in the Bay Area, he had happily passed the story on to friends for many years. He wondered whether it had ever reached Stern.

He'd come by the story, he explained, thanks to another contemporary, whose father, a Mr. Epstein, had been a house painter, sometime contractor and a fellow member of the Workmen's Circle like his own father. When working on larger projects, Epstein hired a few assistants, in this case including one who was perennially after him to come hear his kid play the violin.

Ordinarily, Epstein found excuses to say no. But one day they finished work unexpectedly early and happened to be in the assistant's neighborhood. With no way to beg off, Epstein and his son followed the assistant home. They found what they estimated to be a ten-year-old practicing. As requested, the boy played for them for half an hour. Unable to contain himself, the boy's father, who, of course, was Solomon Stern, asked Epstein what he thought of his Izakel. As he could hardly help but do, Epstein replied politely that it was a delight—for full authenticity, the original Yiddish word is quoted here—and the boy was a great player. "But a Mischa Elman he'll never be," he added.[11]

Three years after Stern began to play, the conservatory presented "Isaac Stern, 10 Year Old Student of Nathan Abas" in a recital of "works by Corelli, Bach, Wieniawski, Pugnani and Kreisler, and Paganini and Kreisler." Again as might be expected, unspecified connections led from the conservatory to Temple Emanu-El, where he inevitably came to the attention of Cantor Rinder.

From here on, as Stern explained to Potok, "everything came together, and he heard me playing, and suddenly he heard talent. And he knew there was no money for study. And there was hardly any money to live on."

Good things were about to happen. But he was or was about to be a school dropout too, and though he may well have been unaware of it, the law that allowed home schooling also required it. A program bio in 1936 reported a taste for math. A visitor from Santa Barbara reported that "he was giving special attention to the study of the French language." What Stern remembered in conversation with Potok were tutors, "some of whom knew something, some of whom didn't." After two years, the authorities noticed his absence and required him to take the Stanford-Binet IQ test, a recent innovation. Mandatory attendance ended at sixteen. His score was what was expected of a sixteen-year-old. It was the end of his formal education.

Meanwhile, someone had to pick up the check. As so often, the dots led back to Rinder. For most of his life, Stern would enjoy the support of formidable women. Only a few steps behind his mother, Lutie Goldstein led the parade. Like so many of the city's German-Jewish gentry, her family was a pillar of Temple Emanu-El, as it was of the conservatory. She lived with a sister at the Fairmont Hotel. Stern remembered a Cadillac and chauffeur. It can be assumed that she was recruited by Rinder. She took on the Stern account with the same patrician self-assurance that the Zellerbach family brought to Fleisher's.

Goldstein's family had made its fortune in packaged dried fruits, as the Zellerbachs had made theirs in paper products. As a dedicated civic activist and patron of the arts, born among the last of eleven children in 1866, she cultivated more fruits. On her death in 1954, there were bequests among others to Brandeis University, the Hebrew University, a medley of local and Jewish charities, and the San Francisco Symphony. As a music-loving civic spirit, she had long since supported the orchestra, opera and every chamber ensemble in the area. "But every San Franciscan knows that Isaac Stern has been Lutie Goldstein's 'pet project,' for the past several years," the *San Francisco News* reported in 1941.

It was her idea to send him to New York, accompanied by his mother, to study with the American-born but European-trained Louis Persinger, who had taught Menuhin and Ricci while concertmaster in San Francisco. Stern recalled the ferry ride to Oakland, the long ride across the continent, the inevitable change of trains in Chicago, and "a honey of a man," who could play the piano part of whatever Stern happened to be working on. What he did *not* play, he remembered, were the etudes by the Viennese Jakob Dont, and the scale regimen—in single notes, thirds, sixths, octaves, fingered octaves, tenths and harmonics—of the iconic Carl Flesch that most violin teachers considered the curricular equivalent of spinach. He met Persinger for lessons three or four times a month. What seems to have impressed him most was his teacher's undemanding amiability, which "was not what I needed at the time."

When the money ran out after six months, he and his mother went home, where it seemed likely that he would return to the conservatory and resume where he had left off. He was now thirteen.

Instead, good things happened again. "I was lucky, very, very, very lucky," he told Potok. It was clear he'd gone as far as the conservatory could take him. "Had I continued on the basis of the training I received in those early years, I would never have found the right road to a concert career," he told a British writer who wanted to know why he forgot or neglected to mention his former teacher, Pollak, in the program notes for a recent concert.

The game changer, as usual, was Lutie Goldstein. As one of the orchestra's most dependable patrons, Goldstein naturally knew Monteux, who had just hired Naoum Blinder as his concertmaster. A native of Odessa, Blinder had left the Soviet Union for a concert tour of Japan. He then continued on to San Francisco, where he agreed to teach Stern, who remembered him ever after as "the teacher who taught me to teach myself, which is the greatest thing a teacher can do."

His method, as Stern recalled it, was conventional practice

in reverse. "He taught me to distrust anyone who prescribed exercises the way a doctor prescribes an aspirin," Stern told an unusually thoughtful interviewer from *Paris Match* as he was approaching seventy. Rather than prescribe fingerings and bowings, he left them for Stern to figure out for himself, intervening only where he thought correction was indicated. Stern learned by his mistakes, Blinder told *Musical America* in 1957.

As a San Franciscan, across the bay from Oakland, he also had occasion to make the acquaintance of the Budapest Quartet, then in residence at Mills College, and the first five of what would be six Bartók quartets that most of the musical world had yet to discover. Above all, there was Alexander Schneider, at the time the quartet's second violinist, and what would grow into a lifelong friendship that would only end with Schneider's death in 1993 and a will that named Stern as one of his three executors.

As Blinder's student, Stern had automatic entry to orchestra rehearsals. Better still, he was invited to play chamber music once or twice a week with Blinder's colleagues, the orchestra's string principals, probably at Blinder's home. He recalled these evenings in part for the music, in part for piles of food. Old enough to be big brothers, if not his father, the players treated him like a colleague, with all that implied. "Whenever they would hear me doing something wrong, they would lace into me like nothing you ever saw," he recalled. "They were without pity—something for which I am thankful today."

It was clearly a formative experience, still noticeable in the so-called Encounters of his final years. Spectators, unfamiliar with the medium, sometimes cringed, and occasional participants even cried, as he did unto a new generation of young players as those long-ago orchestra players had done unto him.

He stayed with Blinder till he was fifteen. Blinder and his wife had a daughter approximately Stern's age, who had died at eleven. "I became a kind of surrogate child to them both in the years that I studied with him, 1932–37," he explained to Sol Schoenbach, a colleague he'd known as principal bassoonist in Philadelphia. As might be expected, he returned to San Francisco in 1965 to play Bach at Blinder's funeral. He again played Bach as a tribute after a performance of the Beethoven concerto a few months later with what for so many years had been Blinder's orchestra.

Though not, *not*, NOT a prodigy, as he never missed an opportunity to repeat, he was already something of a public figure. As early as 1931, he qualified as newsworthy when the *San Francisco Chronicle* announced that "another in the long series of San Francisco's gifted child musicians will make his debut Tuesday evening, when the San Francisco Conservatory of Music sponsors Isaac Stern, 10 year old violin pupil of Nathan Abas, in a mature artist's program at the Sorosis Club Hall."

A year later and now fully eleven, he qualified for a soulful photo of himself with violin in one column in the *Call-Bulletin*. Not only had "his violin recital last night at the Community Playhouse proved that he belongs to the higher order of precocious talents," the *Chronicle* reported, but "a large audience greeted his display with appreciative enthusiasm . . ."

In 1934, "Isaac Stern, boy violinist" moved up another rung, when the Commonwealth Club of California invited him to perform in a club musicale. Two years older than Rotary, the club was founded in 1903 as a place where the local establishment could hear current opinion-makers air the great issues of the day. From 1924, its sessions were broadcast locally, then nationally.

The club newsletter is a time capsule of what else was going on during a week when members gathered on a Thursday evening to hear the still-thirteen-year-old Master Stern share an evening with the club's orchestra, men's chorus and a contralto, then sat down the next day to lunch at $1.00 a plate. With the Depression already in its fifth year, and both the New Deal and the Third Reich in their second, there was no shortage of things to talk about.

Peter H. Odegard, a visiting political science professor at Berkeley with a serious interest in "the fine art of propaganda," talked "rather bluntly and positively," among other things, about "Congress and the Supreme Court, communism, fascism and a private army." Professor David P. Barrows, recently returned from a visiting professorship at the University of Berlin, reported that he saw little evidence of physical brutality against Jews. But he anticipated that official anti-Semitism, though mostly legal, would "have a deleterious effect on Germany as a nation before the world." Speakers from Southern Pacific and the Market Street Railway informed the Traffic Hazards section that there had been "an evident increase in high heel accidents" since a recent revival of high heels.

Members could at least go home after the concert without existential angst. "The finest music in a long line of splendid evenings," was "the unanimous judgment of last Thursday's audience as expressed by applause and comments when the meeting drew to a close," the newsletter noted. The audience was full of enthusiasm for its orchestra and chorus. The singer held the audience in rapt enjoyment. But Master—still years from Mister—Stern's performance had apparently been a "You ain't heard nothin' yet" moment, memorable for "a rare technique, exquisite feeling and a sureness both of bow and fingers which would have been outstanding in any violinist of any age or experience."

In 1935, he made his recital debut at Veterans Auditorium with Betty Alexander, an "extraordinarily gentle but firmly helpful" pianist, as he recalled her, and Blinder as partner in Bach's double violin concerto. He then took on the Paganiniesque concerto of Heinrich Wilhelm Ernst, whose intimidating technical challenges he never felt the need or desire to meet again. A year later, he returned to the San Francisco Symphony for a performance of Saint-Saëns's Third Concerto, a crowd-pleasing evergreen, with Willem van den Burg, the orchestra's principal cellist, as conductor, and the Brahms concerto with Monteux. It was the closest approximation yet to a debutante's coming-out party. Radio had become a serious competitor. But multiple newspapers, still the norm, reserved generous column inches for music reviews, and reviewers like the *Chronicle*'s Alfred Frankenstein often enjoyed an authority editorial writers might envy. Coverage of the next Menuhin was as self-evident as coverage of the next DiMaggio.

The word was already making the rounds before a reviewer so much as left the office. Ordinarily, San Francisco's Junior Chamber of Commerce promoted the greater glory of the state and city with beaches and football fields, Jehanne Bietry Salinger, Pierre's mother, pointed out in the *San Francisco Examiner*. But this time a Californian glory was making history. "Isaac Stern, boy violinist," was about to play the Brahms concerto in his debut appearance with the hometown orchestra, Monteux conducting. The concert was to be broadcast nationally with the Jaycees as sponsor. Her story, on three columns, framed a photo of a very young and earnest Stern in a suit and tie looking up respectfully at a beaming Blinder.

The only question, big enough in an age of saturation coverage to keep performers waiting all night for the first edition of the morning papers, was what the reviewers would say afterward. Careers stood or fell on a quotable phrase—or the lack of one.

Beyond anything to date, the reviews were worth any loss of sleep. Only Jehanne Bietry Salinger, his French tutor and a freelance music reviewer, still apostrophized the "boy." Frankenstein now modified "boy prodigy" with "former." The reference to his age was still obligatory. But for the most part, it was a reminder of where the soloist was coming from and his place in the city's ongoing success as a musical incubator.

"Young Stern belied his 16 years and played in the manner of a finished artist," declared Marjorie M. Fisher of the *News* after his first performance with his teacher's orchestra. "It was a professional performance of high order, and Isaac, his teacher, Naoum Blinder and the city itself are to be congratulated upon his success."

Marie Hicks Davidson of the *Call-Bulletin* reported "a spontaneous ovation accorded him, an outburst prolonged and hearty and punctuated with bravos." Alexander Fried of the *Examiner*, noting his "fiery confidence," enjoined his readers to "keep your eye on Isaac Stern," and hailed "the skill of a full-grown virtuoso." Frankenstein, in the *Chronicle*, hailed "a young man who plays like a house afire, a dry wooden house caught aflame in a high gale."

His solo recital some weeks later again caused Frankenstein to shout "fire" but, as before, it was meant as a compliment. "He has mastered all the technical procedures by which a violin can be made to sound like an accident in a fireworks factory," he wrote, "and while he at times indulged in music that is of no more artistic importance than such a haphazard conflagration, most of his program was devoted to compositions that have something to say." Fisher noted "a program that would challenge the accomplishments of a veteran, and played in a manner that many an established artist might well envy." Fried acknowledged "a recital worthy of a mature master."

At five feet seven, Stern also made his way to Los Angeles, and what was surely a new dimension in looking up to the conductor, for a performance of the Tchaikovsky concerto with the Los Angeles Philharmonic under the six-foot-four-inch Otto Klemperer. Monteux meanwhile addressed a letter to his colleague Vladimir Golschmann in St. Louis. It was a kind of letter he seldom wrote, he emphasized. But in this case he felt it was his duty as a musician.

"A San Francisco boy, seventeen years of age, named Isaac Stern, has just played the Brahms concerto for violin . . . , and I have no hesitation in declaring that he is one of the first truly great violinists of today," he reported. Golschmann would not only be doing Monteux a favor, "and yourself a great pleasure," by signing Stern for the next season. "I feel very sure that he will be a great sensation wherever he plays," Monteux added for good measure.

The last sentence was not entirely wrong. But it was about to be tested. It would be January 1944 before Stern actually made it to St. Louis, and December the same year before he played there with Golschmann. But from there on, it would be almost annual, with thirty-six more appearances to come, the last in 1995.

Meanwhile, there were challenges to meet in 1937. "If I can't make it there, I can't make it anywhere" had been successively true of Paris, London and Berlin. It was now true of New York. A tower of support as always, Lutie Goldstein reappeared to buy him a Guadagnini previously owned by Arma Senkrah, one of the earliest American players of international distinction, and W. H. Winslow, a Chicago amateur, who owned the house that was the young Frank Lloyd Wright's first major commission. Bought for $6,500, it was Stern's first old Italian master. In 1971, on loan to Henry Shweid, an old friend and longtime San Francisco Symphony player, it was appraised by Jacques Francais, the New York dealer, at $25,000. In 1997, it again changed hands, this time for $500,000.[12]

Accompanied by his mother, a rising son boarded the train in Oakland and again set off for the east. In October 1917, Heifetz had made his legendary Carnegie Hall debut at about the same age. Twenty years later to the month, Stern, like most newcomers to New York, made his debut at Town Hall, with at least 1,200 seats compared with Carnegie's 2,800, but wonderful acoustics. As he reminded people all his life, he did not play like

Heifetz. No one could. But he was resolved to be the best possible Isaac Stern.

Someone, he wasn't sure who, had rented the hall, and paid for the tickets, advertising and pianist. The program, a document in itself, carried ads for Steinway, the piano maker, with a blurb of recommendation from Stern; for Wurlitzer, en route to becoming the city's premier violin shop; for upcoming performers from Columbia Concerts; for Schrafft's, a New York institution, with its "Fine Food, Fine Sodas and Fine Cocktails," and for the Beresford, "the aristocrat of Central Park West," where he would both live and maintain a combination office-studio for much of his life.

Free tickets, letters from friends at home to friends in New York, and news of his West Coast successes apparently produced a large audience. He played in a suit. After the concert, he assumed, he'd gone out to eat, since that was his habit. He then bought the early editions of the morning papers.

The reviewers had showed up in battalion strength, with the quasi-papal Olin Downes of the *New York Times* prominent among them. Though no names were named, Stern had somewhere got the impression that Downes had come under pressure from unspecified "people of influence" and was not entirely happy about another evening at Town Hall.

The reviews at best fell short of expectation. With thirteen reviewer-friendly column inches at his disposal, Downes noted Stern's left hand as well as his "clean and manly intent." But he missed "the consistent beauty and resiliency of tone which should be his." Like a middle school teacher conferring with a concerned mother at a PTA meeting, he nonetheless acknowledged "unusual potential as an artist," and added reassuringly that "self-criticism and maturity can carry him far."

Irving Kolodin, writing in the *Sun*, saw Stern as the latest evidence that good violinists were as prevalent in California as oranges. But while he agreed that the latest Californian showed "indubitable talent," he "was not wholly convinced that he has actually traversed the Great Divide that separates the promising player from the artist." R.C.B. in the *World-Telegram* reported at least that the newcomer from "that far away land of violinist prodigies, movie 'yes-men' and sunshine" had "definite possibilities." Francis D. Perkins, with thirteen column inches in the *Herald Tribune*, anticipated that "an unusually promising young musician whose talent seems to be following a normal and judicious course of development, should become an artist of exceptional consequence in the fairly near future." Samuel Chotzinoff, Heifetz's brother-in-law, saw "the makings of a fine player, but he should watch himself and listen carefully to some of his colleagues."

Back in San Francisco, Fisher of the *News* pointed with civic pride to Kolodin's recognition of the latest California orange. She also quoted a collegial letter of congratulations from Persinger to Blinder. "I attended the recital, of course," Persinger wrote, "and one of the things that impressed me most was Isaac's APPROACH . . . , the SPIRIT, I mean." The boy showed "a musical SOUL," he continued. He was happy to see "that San Francisco has not given up producing REAL violinists!"

But this was little comfort to Stern three time zones away. The next day he boarded a double-decker bus on Fifth Avenue and rode up and down Manhattan Island. Meanwhile, his increasingly frantic mother, without a clue where he had gone, called everyone she knew and considered a call to the police.

It was a "to be or not to be" moment. Was it nobler in the mind to hang in there and take his chances on the concert career he wanted above all else, or to take the concertmaster job offered by any of the many radio orchestras then in flower, and earn $150 a week, more money to support his family than he had ever dreamed of? It was six hours before he got off the bus with his answer.

At first his parents were angry, he told Potok, but they came around. The message was bumper-sticker simple. "I had to prove," he explained. "I worked like hell to hone my skills with Blinder." It meant practicing till everything became nearly automatic, teaching hands and fingers to know where to go and what it feels like, learning to do what once took three days in three hours, plus playing and playing for Blinder, conductors, and anyone else who would listen.

There were also concerts, minor league exhibitions in their way, like recitals in Seattle and Palo Alto. An expansive feature in the *Seattle Times* noted his fondness for large steaks, substantial breakfasts and tennis that coexisted with five hours of daily practice, tutorials in the basic high school subjects, and a salad lunch. "I went away feeling that I'd been assisting in the preliminary career of a world celebrity," wrote John D. Barry of the *San Francisco News*, who'd come north to hear him with a good-sized contingent of hometown fans.

A consortium of fourteen Jewish patrons meanwhile collected

$2,350 in personal donations to help see him back to his rendezvous with destiny, again at Town Hall. "Like most of San Francisco's musical prodigies, including the now affluent Yehudi, he comes from poor parents, who lavished on him, however, a wealth of genius and a world of care," the Temple Emanu-El Journal reported in what was now March 1938. "Our pride in our tradition, particularly at a time when music is prized as a boon to nerve-ridden mankind, and our affection for Isaac, modest and lovable, should command a support from the community that will help him find the highest fulfillment of his great gift."

In February 1939, not yet nineteen, Stern returned to New York by air. It was the first of what were to be countless flights. This time no one called him a boy. His performance "established his title to mature mastery," G.G. told readers of the *New York Times*." He was "among the most important violinists now to be heard," J.D.B. told readers of the *Herald Tribune*. "Violin playing of uncommon technical solidity and musical distinction," said Irving Kolodin in the *Sun*. "There was in everything that he played an earnestness and intensity which were the marks of fine musicianship," said S. in *Musical America*.

"The result was like day and night," he told Potok. "I was suddenly accepted." A decade after setting out as apprentice, he'd checked the final box en route to master. He was now a professional, an American professional, on the threshold of a career that would extend, practically uninterrupted, across the remainder of Luce's American Century.

II

# Professional

"EVERYTHING IN WAR IS SIMPLE," CLAUSEWITZ observed, "but even the simplest things are difficult." He could as well have been talking about being a concert violinist. Stern had practiced, practiced, practiced. But he still had miles to go before he got to Carnegie Hall.

By definition, the job called for an artist. But it also called for an entertainer with Ironman stamina, a diplomat with a nose for politics, a miniature CEO with a marketable product, and ideally a medley of any or all of these. Stern had already checked off many of the boxes. But whether and how he checked off the rest depended still more on time, place, an impressively diverse support group extending both east and west across three oceans and, as always, luck.

In 1928, Carl Flesch, a respected performer as well as one of the era's most respected teachers, published a manual about virtually everything an aspiring violinist might want to know and was afraid to ask. The proper position of wrist and elbow? How to manage stage fright, perspiration before the coming of antiperspirants, enthusiastic—and overenthusiastic—fans? It was all there in two volumes.

Decades would pass before Stern even became aware of it, and that only because C. F. Flesch, the author's son, acting on a nudge from the musicologist Boris Schwarz, presented him a copy. "You can imagine how valuable such a book is to someone who is eternally a student of the violin,—as we must all be if we are still serious," Stern replied gracefully.[1] But what could it tell him that he didn't already know after thirty years in the business? Without knowing it, he'd been acting it out more comprehensively than any other player since it first appeared, and probably having more fun.

But at this point the fun still lay ahead, and the difficulties that Clausewitz called friction were just beginning. "Think of the traveler with two more stops to make before dark, and four or five more hours on the road" Clausewitz continues. "He arrives at the last stop but one, finds bad horses or none, then mountains, bad roads, dark of night, and is grateful to reach the last stop with effort and find a roof for the night."

Substitute the systemic vagaries of trains, planes, wind, weather, hotels and airports 160 to 200 times a year. Learn to accommodate the stolen, misplaced, mistaken, damaged and forgotten luggage that Arnold Steinhardt, cofounder and longtime first violinist of the Guarneri Quartet, recalled with the authority of one who had also been there and done that.[2] Include the one-night stands and absence from home at dinnertime, the heady expectations of parents, teachers and patrons, and the sink-or-swim imperatives of the debut recital. Add a competition circuit that extended the intramural rigors of the nineteenth-century Paris Conservatory not only to Brussels, Moscow, Hannover,

Genoa and Indianapolis over the course of Stern's lifetime, but to Shanghai and a generously endowed new competition there, posthumously dedicated to Stern himself.

Factor for irregular and eccentric school attendance; the need to find and ideally bond with a compatible pianist, cultivate conductors, and persuade managers that they need you at least as much as you need them. If Russian, adapt to an opaque and arbitrary bureaucracy that told you where you could and couldn't go and took a generous cut for its services. An assistant who venerated him recalled that even the great David Oistrakh was afraid of dying poor. If on your own, make your own deals as an enterprise of one, with collateral expenses including a pianist as well as travel, meals and lodging, in a cultural ecosystem that provides neither a dependable nest egg, a safety net nor a parachute. Enter managers, concert presenters and record producers, lawyers, financial advisors, investment counselors, haberdashers, dressmakers, travel agents, podiatrists and physical therapists, whose services literally extend from head to foot.

Add contingencies of time and place, twin icebergs waiting for a *Titanic*, that would challenge the most resourceful of insurance adjusters. There were the recalcitrant piano in Shanghai, the open seam in India, with no shop available to fix it,[3] and at least two Middle East wars, that appeared uninvited in Stern's working life. There was the orchestra strike in Detroit that complicated Sarah Chang's. There were the instrument burglars who made life miserable for itinerant virtuosi from Ludwig Spohr and Eugène Ysaÿe to Bronislaw Huberman, Roman Totenberg and Pierre Amoyal, as well as the heirs and executors of Erica Morini.

There were the political tectonics that diverted the lives and careers of Mischa Elman, Efrem Zimbalist, Jascha Heifetz and Nathan Milstein, let alone their teacher Leopold Auer, from St. Petersburg to points west, including New York and Los Angeles, and upended Szymon Goldberg's career as precocious concertmaster of the Berlin Philharmonic. There were the nearly lethal misadventures—a plane crash and wartime internment respectively—that befell both Huberman and Goldberg in Indonesia; the alcohol, drugs and depression that prematurely ended the careers of Eugene Fodor, Michael Rabin and Christian Ferras; the focal dystonia that devastated the career of Stern's friend and colleague Leon Fleisher and nearly did the same to his friend and colleague Leonard Rose. There was the carpal tunnel syndrome that even afflicted Stern himself in his final years. There was the car crash that killed Ossy Renardy. There were the air crashes that killed Ginette Neveu and Jacques Thibaud en route to concert engagements. Renardy's violin, at least, survived. Neveu's and Thibaud's did not.

"Immortality is not for everyone," says a character in *Der Gross-Cophta*, one of Goethe's least known comedies. It is unlikely that Stern knew the play. But he had no need for Goethe to be aware of the message.

From the earliest Baroque superstar to the latest Asian whiz kid, it was axiomatic that the successful soloist was a player who could do what others couldn't. The items on the soloist's check list could be anticipated at any distance and were unlikely to come as a surprise. Exceptional fine motor skills and superior pitch discrimination invariably topped the list. But as Stern never tired of emphasizing, temperament, personality and character, irrespective of luck and elbows, were at least as essential. "You have to be arrogant to walk out in front of an audience and say shut up and listen . . . ," he told Potok. "You can't apologize for being on stage. You have to say 'I'm here now. Be quiet. I'm going to tell you something.' "

Yet none of these, alone or in combination, sufficed in itself to explain, let alone produce, a Paganini or a Heifetz. Talent, and perhaps especially talent of their magnitude, needed to be recognized, guided and developed. It then had to be marketed and equipped.

The self-taught virtuoso is as improbable as the self-taught surgeon or physicist. Stern honored Blinder all his life for teaching an uncommonly bright and motivated pubescent to teach himself. But this was not to be taken literally. What was meant, as Stern unfailingly acknowledged, was that Blinder encouraged him to try things, then told him what worked, what didn't and proposed alternatives where indicated.

It was no less axiomatic that a violinist needs a violin. Whether it was a product of Cremona in 1720 or of Brooklyn in living memory was a matter for player, seller and bank to negotiate among themselves. What was not negotiable was an instrument, irrespective of origin, that could be heard even pianissimo over an orchestra of 120 on all five levels in all 2,804 seats of Carnegie Hall. With rarest exceptions, the traveling pianist makes do with what's available in the local hall. Save for the occasional string break where the concertmaster is needed as first responder, the itinerant violinist plays personal property, chosen at least as carefully as a marriage partner.

Like Paganini, many players collected instruments for fun and potential profit. But where their concert instrument was concerned, they tended to monogamy. Paganini lived only briefly with the mother of his son and never married at all. But he remained devoted to the del Gesù, still on display in Genoa, for most of his life. Heifetz married twice, yet remained faithful to the del Gesù now on display in San Francisco. Stern, who married three times, played two del Gesùs for most of his life. His relationship to both of them lasted considerably longer than two of the three marriages. Ysaÿe, a previous owner of one of the two, declared it the faithful companion of his life. So did Stern.

Necessity begat more necessities. A luthier and most usually a dealer were needed to sell and service the violin. A cash reserve was needed to buy, and a bank, patron or other creditor to finance, or a friendly collector to loan a capital investment, whose dollar-denominated price would grow from four digits to seven over Stern's working lifetime.

Like the teacher's, the dealer's and luthier's services needed to be paid for too. Franz von Vecsey, a son of the prewar Hungarian gentry, and Albert Spalding, son of an emblematic sporting goods entrepreneur and nephew of a pioneer Chicago Cub, came from families that could pay their way. But they were exceptional. For their peers from Odessa, Vilna and San Francisco, patrons and scholarships were one more necessary condition.

The market imposed still more conditions. When negotiating where, what and how much, artists, managers and concert presenters relate to one another like tenants and landlords. But asked whether the falling tree makes a sound in the absence of someone to hear it, they pair as naturally as pitcher and catcher, and their answer is audible and in unison. Since Arcangelo Corelli wowed 'em in Rome and Thomas Baltzar wowed 'em in London, performers have existed to play in public for an audience that pays to hear them. The presenter, like the manager, exists to connect supply and demand.

Meanwhile, a critical mass of composers created a canon that would become and remain the performers' stock in trade. Comprehensive as the piano's for the instrument that most closely approximates the human voice, the literature would extend across music's periodic table, from Monti's *Czárdás* to the Bach Chaconne, with something in principle for everyone.

It was true, if sad, that the Beethoven concerto, like Goethe's immortality, was not for everyone or everywhere. But it was clear by the seventeenth century that demand and supply had something going, and a receptive public grew parallel to the population, GNP and the middle class. Italy, cradle of makers, players and composers, was already a good place to be a concert violinist by the end of the seventeenth century. London, Paris and the German minicapitals had become such places by the end of the eighteenth. With a powerful assist from such players as Niccolò Paganini, Henri Vieuxtemps, Henryk Wieniawski, Joseph Joachim and Pablo de Sarasate, most of Europe had become a happy hunting ground by the end of the nineteenth. Decades before the arrival of the Sterns, America too showed promise.

Yehudi Menuhin and Ruggiero Ricci, Stern's contemporaries and fellow San Franciscans, were evidence enough that he was far from the first American professional. But predecessors of all three had already surfaced by the 1860s, when Camilla Urso appeared in New York and Philadelphia with the ancestors of orchestras that Stern would come to know as friends and colleagues.

French-born and Paris-trained, Urso was thirteen when she arrived in America. But she was clearly at home in 1869, when she played what might have been the first-ever American performance of the Beethoven concerto with the Harvard Musical Association. The Association was still active in 1992, when Harvard awarded Stern an honorary degree.

By this time, everyone played the Beethoven. Decade after decade, Stern himself had not only performed it with orchestras and conductors from Carnegie Hall to Jerusalem; he had also recorded it twice, and was now passing it on to the next generation. He spent two hours coaching his brilliantly talented protégé Pinchas Zukerman on the first twenty measures of the violin entrance alone, he recalled in his memoir. Zukerman left in tears.

Stern could also relate to Urso's calendar. In an era when the stagecoach had only recently given way to the steam locomotive, she played eight concerts, holidays included, between mid-December 1873 and January 1, 1874. Five years later, she reportedly played two hundred for audiences spread across fifteen states and two territories before taking off for California, Australia and New Zealand.

Over the next four decades, at least six more Americans qualified for international attention. Anna Harkness, born in upstate New York in 1864, graduated from the Paris Conservatory with all possible honors at seventeen. Rebranded as Arma Senkrah by

Hermann Wolff, the godfather of modern music management, she triumphed from London to St. Petersburg, played Beethoven sonatas with Franz Liszt, and was named court violinist to the Grand Duke of Saxony before an unfortunate marriage and suicide ended her career at thirty-six.

Born respectively in Washington, D.C., Davenport, Iowa, and Boston, Leonora von Stosch, Florizel von Reuter and Leonora Jackson did fine with the names they were born with. After study in Brussels and Leipzig, Stosch made her Boston Symphony debut at eighteen. Jackson, winner of the Leipzig Conservatory's Mendelssohn scholarship at eight, played the Brahms concerto with the Berlin Philharmonic while still in her teens, and the New York Philharmonic at twenty-one. Reuter, who performed at a precocious age for President McKinley at the White House, was the first to make a full concert program of the 24 Paganini caprices. All three distinguished themselves collaterally too, Stosch as a Pulitzer Prize–winning poet, Reuter as an enthusiastic spiritualist whose Paganini connection extended to the Great Beyond, and Jackson as patron, art collector and a pillar of Washington society.

By this time, Stern's future could be seen coming up over the horizon in the persons of Maud Powell and Albert Spalding. Both were from Chicago. Like their predecessors, both had also decamped for Europe. But their careers, each in its way, were as American as "The Stars and Stripes Forever," which the German-American Max Liebling incidentally arranged for Powell as the kind of encore piece that audiences adore.

Before her premature death at fifty-two, Powell had toured with both the Gilmore and Sousa bands, introduced the Tchaikovsky, Sibelius and Dvořák concertos to the United States, and been known to appear with her quartet every night for five weeks and play two concerts a day while on the road with Sousa. But her most durable legacy was a trail of local orchestras and support groups stretching across a landscape she'd cultivated like a musical Johnny Appleseed, and a stack of Victrola records second only to Caruso's.

Theodore Thomas, the pioneer conductor, offered her a two-year retainer to appear as soloist with his orchestra at $150 a concert. "Maud believed that it was possible to make a good living with the violin, provided the ambitions squared with talent and circumstances," her biographers wrote.[4] This was yet another item Stern would have had no trouble with.

Nor can he have been unaware of Spalding, who was widely recorded and broadcast while Stern was growing up, and remained active until 1950. "America's Violinist," a Carnegie Hall poster proclaimed, and it was no exaggeration. Already a decade into a flourishing international career, Spalding canceled a reported $35,000 worth of concerts to serve in the air force in World War I. He came back with an Italian decoration and resumed where he left off.

In 1941 he played the premiere of Samuel Barber's violin concerto, one that Stern would be first to record. Three years later, Spalding again put his career on hold when Adolf Berle, a social friend and assistant secretary of state, asked him to put his Italian expertise to use as a psychological warfare specialist in North Africa and Italy.

Three years later, Spalding made an understandable impression when he calmed a jittery crowd in a Naples air-raid shelter with a violin someone had happened to bring along. Stern would do something similar when Israel came under fire from Iraq in 1991. In 1953, the year he died, ending a life, a concert career of forty-five years and some two hundred Atlantic crossings, Spalding was inducted into France's Légion d'Honneur. Stern, a transatlantic commuter himself as well as a major collector of official honors including this one, would again have nodded recognition. That Spalding was a serious tennis player like Stern himself was one more item Stern could relate to.

What distinguished him from all previous Americans of international concert class was that they—even Menuhin, who went to Paris to study with Georges Enesco, even Ricci who went to Berlin to study with Georg Kulenkampff—had looked to Europe as their finishing school. Stern, who had lived in the United States without interruption since babyhood, was the first world-class player who had not.

The distinction was a perennial object of interest to interviewers. The great European teachers had come to America, he replied when asked—and not Israel, as he added in an interview with Myriam Anissimov in *Le Monde de la Musique* in 1984.[5] In effect, Europe had come to him.

What went unmentioned, most probably because mention was unnecessary, was that the Europeans had not only come, but had stayed. Since at least the 1960s, Juilliard, Curtis and Indiana University were as much the new Paris, Brussels and Leipzig for young Europeans like Ulf Hoelscher, Christian Tetzlaff and

Pierre Amoyal and young Asians like Kyung Wha Chung, Cho-Liang (aka Jimmy) Lin and Takako Nishizaki, as they were for young Americans like Joshua Bell and Hilary Hahn.

Israel, of course, was a case unto itself, not least thanks to Stern. Brilliant young talent that would once have gravitated to Auer's studio in St. Petersburg, to Joachim and Flesch in Berlin or the Paris Conservatory, now gravitated to Ivan Galamian, who himself had made it to New York via Tabriz, Moscow and Paris. His protégée and successor, Dorothy DeLay of Medicine Lodge, Kansas, Oberlin Conservatory and Michigan State, could not have been more American. The young American who wanted to go to Europe was no longer even quite certain where to go.

Asked which of the various schools—Italian, French, Belgian, German, Czech, Russian—he considered his own, Stern refused to identify with any of them. Schools meant rules, and rules meant limitations, he told Joseph Wechsberg of *The New Yorker*. "There should be no limitations except those imposed by taste."[6]

For himself, the question of provenance had been literally academic since his Town Hall breakthrough. It had been clear since he was eight that he was unusually gifted. But there was plenty of talent around, he told Wechsberg, and there were more bad musicians than there was bad music. Talent was not sufficient. There were still those necessary conditions. A decade later, he had satisfied many of the most important conditions: talent, temperament, teacher, instrument, patron. But there were still more waiting, including the basic challenges of where to find an audience and how to connect with it. Until then, the question of where he was going was more equal than all others, and this could also be understood literally.

It would soon become clear and remain clear for the remainder of his life that Stern had satisfied one more condition by arriving in the right country at the right time. Maud Powell and civic spirit had left their marks. There were an estimated 17 American orchestras before World War I, according to one survey. There were 270 in 1939.[7]

Beginning in 1930, the New York Philharmonic broadcast every Sunday on Columbia Broadcasting System's national network. In 1937, the music-loving David Sarnoff created an elite NBC Symphony to broadcast Saturday evenings on his National Broadcasting Company network. As Spalding noted presciently, the war in Europe, then in its second month, added its bit by turning America into "the last remaining musical market."[8]

But the boom was already under way before the war. By the 1940s, both networks had spun off concert series, respectively Civic Concerts and Columbia Arts Management Inc. (CAMI), that reached out to some 2,000 communities, as well as record companies with labels that would become as familiar as Macy's and Gimbels. It continued afterward as 2 million veterans crowded America's colleges and universities, and some 300 college concert series too became part of the cultural landscape. Between 1932 and 1952, according to another survey, the North American concert audience had doubled, and there were three times as many concerts in the United States and Canada per annum as in the rest of the world put together.[9] Audiences had matured as well as grown, Stern observed in conversation with Wechsberg.

In a very different era, a fully adult Paganini had entertained an audience that couldn't get enough of him as music's version of the Flying Wallendas, with left-hand pizzicati and double harmonics no one to date believed possible, as well as an occasional display of animal imitations. Stern, at age eighteen, opened a demonstratively grown-up debut recital with Brahms's d minor sonata and Bach's d minor solo partita in all movements en route to the monumental chaconne.

But pragmatism, where indicated, also did the job. "Playing for the most discriminating audience . . . ," the local paper reported a few weeks later from Pensacola, Florida, "Isaac Stern, 18-year-old Californian of Russian birth, rendered flawlessly a program drawn from a virtuoso repertoire." He was "obliged to respond with several encores," the reviewer added.

"It was evident that no intricacies of bowing or fingering baffled this young artist," was the word from Janesville, Wisconsin. "His playing was so effortless and he seemed to be enjoying himself so thoroughly that his audience responded in like manner."

"Chatting affably before the performance, the young San Franciscan disclosed himself as an enthusiastic musician, typically American for all he was born in Russia," the *Manchester Leader* noted approvingly. "He likes traveling about the country and finds New Hampshire delightful in its contrast to the west coast . . ."

Ten days later, sponsored by the local chapter of B'nai B'rith, he was in Vancouver at the other end of the continent to play a benefit for German refugees "regardless of race or religion." A two-column newspaper photo showed him in earnest conversation with the mayor, who was to join him later in the day for a broadcast interview.

Within two weeks, he had covered Florida, New Hampshire, Wisconsin and British Columbia in an era when air travel was glamorous, expensive and uncommon and jet air travel as yet unimaginable. "Wherever I played, the reviews were excellent," he recalled. "There was nothing I could learn from them," he added. "Still. How I reveled in the good reviews." Both literally and professionally, he was on his way, leaving behind a trail of new friends and connections.

Two new connections in particular added value to a growth stock. But it was a growth stock the market had yet to discover.

The first connection was a new pianist. Russian-born and eighteen years Stern's senior, Alexander Zakin was a graduate of the Berlin Hochschule für Musik, where he had studied along with Stern's current pianist, Leopold Mittman. In 1940 he arrived in New York just as Mittman was about to accept a better offer from Mischa Elman. Mittman recommended his classmate, Zakin. Stern put him on an annual salary, with negotiated supplements for radio, TV and recordings. So far as he knew, the relationship was unique. They would remain together till Zakin's health collapsed thirty-seven years later.

The second connection was new management. It was true that they loved him in Pensacola and Janesville. But neither the *Pensacola Journal* nor the *Janesville Daily Gazette* was widely read outside of Pensacola and Janesville respectively, and the market for eighteen-year-old violinists made in the USA was not bullish.

By the end of 1939, the one-way ticket to the salaried orchestra job he had spurned in 1937 looked increasingly attractive. In two years, his contract with the National Concert and Artists agency (NCAC), an affiliate of NBC and parent of Civic Concerts, had brought him only six or seven concerts. Yet only a few months later, the sky brightened over Lake Michigan. A successful debut with the Chicago Symphony in early 1940 was bound to boost anyone's morale. He had also found, and been found by, a new manager who saw the potential NBC hadn't. By 1941, he was on a third national tour and his calendar included some thirty concerts, both with orchestra and in recital with Zakin.

The tiebreaker and second crucial connection was Paul Stoes, who had himself set out to be a violinist. In a previous life, Stoes had both studied and taught at Chicago's Bush Conservatory, the creation of a local piano maker and retailer in 1901. A century later, the six-story French Renaissance building with piano showroom, theater, museum and clock tower that once housed it, was declared a Chicago landmark. But its creators had failed to factor in the Great Depression.

In 1932, it surrendered its identity in a merger with a more viable institution, and Stoes had evidently reconsidered his vocation. By the time he discovered Stern eight years later, he had established himself as an independent agent with a small but respectable list of clients and lateral connections including the Don Cossack Choir, the Vienna Boys Choir, Igor Stravinsky and Fritz Kreisler. Stoes, who had every reason to believe that Stern would become a moneymaker, personally chauffeured him from engagement to engagement on the kind of highways the writer

William Least Heat-Moon evocatively called blue. But his expectations, while great, were also premature.

Though appalled by Stoes's politics and raucous conversation, Stern was well aware of what he owed him. "He gave me my basic grounding in the business end of music, and encouraged me to continue when I needed it most," he told Roland Gelatt of *High Fidelity*.[10] He was also wistfully grateful to Stoes for a dinner in Philadelphia with Fritz Kreisler, already one of Stern's heroes as an artist. In the absence of his famously imperious wife, Kreisler delivered a tutorial, course by course and wine by wine, on how a serious European gentleman eats and drinks. Stern would remember it ever after.[11]

Stoes's problem, and therefore Stern's problem, was cash flow. It was unlikely that the Choir Boys, last heard in New York in 1938, the year Nazi Germany annexed their country, would be seen again anytime soon. The Don Cossacks were an easy sell. But they were also his only dependable moneymaker, and too little to keep his shop in independent operation.

At this point, as it frequently did in Stern's life, luck intervened. The scenario was reminiscent of the midwinter baseball meetings where a promising left-handed closer is exchanged for To Be Announced (TBA) and an unspecified bundle of cash. Stoes's network was extensive, but deficient in glamour. Sol Hurok's list included a startling number of the era's superstars. Their merger, if not exactly made in heaven, was certainly a marriage of convenience.

Hurok, in turn, with a lifelong passion for Russian performers, was keen to acquire the Don Cossacks. Stoes, who was not exactly bargaining from strength, agreed to Hurok's takeover. But he managed to include Stern, whom Hurok had never heard of, in the role of TBA, and what began as a blind date soon morphed into a relationship that was at once paternal and win-win.

Both Stern and Hurok spoke bad Russian, disliked Germany, favored good food and wine, and were deeply committed to the violin. Both had a feel for politics and a nose for talent. Each regarded himself with good reason as a walking personification of the American Dream. The first five years of the relationship were contractual. But from there to the end, they carried on by handshake. Neither had reason to regret it.

Hurok's death in 1974, Stern would recall in his memoir, was like the loss of a parent. He remained with the agency for another two years; meanwhile, the sale of the agency to a new owner, followed by a mass exodus of artists, eventually led the company into bankruptcy proceedings that were still in progress in 1990. For the moment, he trod contractual water with engagements booked before the Hurok agency self-destructed.[12] He then rejoined ICM Artists, Ltd., a creation of Hurok alumni, including his former secretary, Lee Lamont, who was now CEO of her own agency. A formidable figure in her own right, she would play managerial bad cop on his behalf for the remainder of his career.[13]

But this, of course, was decades ahead. It was now 1943. Since 1939, the Stern family had been living in New York. Their apartment on West End Avenue was in walking distance of Carnegie Hall and the Beresford apartments at 81st Street and Central Park West. Both would become major compass points in Stern's life and career. Meanwhile, he was preparing for the Carnegie Hall debut that would be his moment of truth.

At first, he moved in with a hospitable married couple, music-loving, comfortably well off and old enough to be his parents. He then moved in with Hyman H. Goldsmith, a physics professor at City College, whose apartment was a convenient practice room during the day when Goldsmith was teaching, and a congenial place for Stern to eat, socialize and play chamber music with Goldsmith's musician friends at night. Loosely associated with the Manhattan Project, Goldsmith would become a founder and coeditor of the *Bulletin of the Atomic Scientists*.

Rather a speed bump than a watershed, America's entry in World War II found Stern performing in locations as disparate as San Angelo and Texarkana, Texas; Minot, North Dakota; Pittsburgh; Cincinnati and San Francisco. Preceded by the emblematic "S. Hurok Presents," his moment finally arrived in early January 1943, and after that everything was different.

"When I started playing in the late 1930's, it was still the fashion to some degree to play concerti with piano accompaniment and lots of petits fours at the end," he told Hurok's biographer years later. By coincidence, Heifetz was in town the same day to play just such a program as a benefit for the Vassar College Scholarship Fund at the Metropolitan Opera House. A "large and fervently demonstrative audience" showed up to hear it, the *New York Times* reported the next day in two short paragraphs.

But it was Stern, in a full outside column of six long paragraphs, who qualified as the day's big story. His program could hardly have been more different from Heifetz's. "I went through half of the violin literature in one afternoon!" he recalled, as though reviewing himself ex post facto. "It was an endless and silly program, but it started things moving."

The part of the sentence that followed the comma was hard to quarrel with. But there was nothing silly about the first of the Bach solo sonatas, Mozart's Schubertian K. 304, and Brahms's practically symphonic sonata in d minor. Each, from successive epochs of music history, was there to make his point, that the violin exists for the sake of the music, and not the other way around. Reservations notwithstanding, he then added two Polish concertos in piano reduction. The first, Henryk Wieniawski's second, first performed in 1862, was obviously meant as a crowd-pleaser. The second, Karol Szymanowski's second, composed in 1932–33, made a corollary statement, that the literature of the violin had a present, even a future, as well as a past.

Over time, the Bach would recede. Within a few years, the piano reductions, a nineteenth-century artifact that he deplored as musically and aesthetically wrong, would vanish too. As Stern saw it, he was kicking off "a whole trend away from some pianist making a massacre of the orchestral part in a violin recital." Hurok feared for the box office. Stern was adamant. "I want to play music," he fired back.

He made his point. "Concertos with piano replacing the orchestra were happily conspicuous by their absence," Olin Downes of the *New York Times* noted approvingly on Stern's return to Carnegie in December 1945.[14] The Brahms d minor sonata, on the other hand, remained uncontested, "a work that could serve as

Mr. Stern's signature tune,"[15] Downes's successor Donal Henahan noted in 1987. Beyond any of his contemporaries and most of his younger colleagues, Stern also remained open and accessible to living composers till the end of his career.

"Endless and silly" as his program looked to him in later years, its logic was still plausible when he recalled it in his memoir. "I selected pieces that would serve as the necessary reaffirmation of the reason I was a musician," he explained. "I played almost defiantly to demonstrate my skills, to show them all what I was capable of doing with the fiddle."

It evidently worked. The *Herald Tribune*'s reviewer found the Szymanowski "tempestuous," and didn't like its "hubbub" and "little tantrums." But even he acknowledged "a musician of fine sensibility and superb technique."[16] Stern, "who held the interest of a large gathering . . . in a formidable program," delivered "an evening of definitely distinguished violin playing," the *New York Times* reported.[17] There was no mention by anyone of "endless" or "silly."

To Stern's gratification, Irving Kolodin of the *New York Sun* also got the intended message. The program "would have appalled most of the case-hardened virtuosi," he wrote, "but Mr. Stern survived the challenge he set for himself with imposing dexterity and musical resourcefulness."[18] Even the famously censorious Virgil Thomson hailed "this ebullient violinist with the big juicy tone and abundance of quotable quips."

Carnegie Hall "was my musical-coming-of-age, my professional bar mitzvah," he told Potok. Since 1937, he had worked his way up through the minors. He was now a major-leaguer.

In principle, he was also eligible for the draft. But he was disqualified for service by a combination of flat feet and a pilonidal sinus, a minor but infection-prone birth defect at the base of the spine, known to Army doctors as jeep disease. Instead, as he was reminded nearly sixty years later by a fan letter from Jean Spencer Felton,[19] the intern who changed the dressing, he had the sinus surgically repaired. He then volunteered for two tours with the United Service Organizations (USO), a congressionally chartered federation of private support groups, created to support the social and practical needs of military personnel and their families. Like Felton, who would go on to a distinguished career in occupational medicine,[20] Stern then went about his own career.

By the time the war was over, he had played some fifty concerts in the United States and Canada, including performances with the Philadelphia Orchestra and the New York Philharmonic. Given the contingencies and priorities of wartime travel, his itinerary alone—Cleveland, Columbus and Akron, Ohio; Fort Worth, Houston, Laredo and Waco, Texas; Cedar Falls, Iowa; Stamford, Connecticut; Boston, Massachusetts; Joplin and Kansas City, Missouri; Omaha, Nebraska; Madison, Wisconsin; Niagara Falls and New Rochelle, New York; Perth Amboy, New Jersey; as well as Ottawa, Montreal and Quebec City—was a thing of wonder.

"In some ways, the war years were heady, free-wheeling times," Stern recalled. The postwar years would only get headier, not least for himself. What had only recently been the worst of times showed promise of becoming the best.

America was now the country where the future began. Its

military might was unequaled. Its currency was to the global economy what the sun was to the solar system. Between 1940 and 1960, its GNP had grown from some $200 billion to $500 billion. A tidal surge of discretionary income, higher education and technical innovation—commercial air travel, FM radio, and the long-playing (LP) record—also meant easier access to more and bigger audiences for American artists and American culture, even in places that till now had shown little interest in either.

Between September and December 1945, Stern had already played twenty concerts. By 1947, he was reportedly playing ninety concerts a year at $1,000–$1,500 and up.[21] By the end of 1953, after thirteen years together, he estimated that he and Zakin had already "traveled hundreds of thousands of miles, nearly all of it by air."[22] By 1990 his frequent flier account, an aggregate of nine airlines, stood at 267,516 miles, enough to take him almost eleven times around the world.

His fees too—somewhere in the $20,000s for a weekend with Washington's National Symphony in the 1970s, $60,000 for four performances of the Beethoven concerto with the Chicago Symphony in the 1990s—had long since reached the stratosphere. The tenor Luciano Pavarotti and pianist Vladimir Horowitz earned the kind of fees more generally associated with twenty-game winners, Super Bowl quarterbacks and the Beatles. They were followed by the singers, Joan Sutherland and Leontyne Price. But then came the instrumentalists, and of the violinists only Itzhak Perlman, Stern's discovery and protégé, matched Stern's cruising altitude.[23]

To the delight of John Kongsgaard, a Napa Valley vintner and impresario of a summer chamber series, Stern was also delighted to play for ten cases of Kongsgaard's wine.[24] Meanwhile, as a gesture of esteem and gratitude for Stern's help in finding his daughter a serious violin teacher, Dr. Yune-Gill Jeong, a Chattanooga pulmonologist, kept him supplied with Vidalia onions.

Since 1945, he had also recorded regularly for Columbia. At first, the medium was easily breakable shellac disks that played at most five minutes of music at 78 rpm. Beginning in 1949, there was a watershed transition to virtually indestructible vinyl. Cautiously introduced and soon ubiquitous, the LP was good for at least twenty minutes at 33⅓ rpm. Since 1958 it had even been available in stereo. In 1982, Philips and Sony introduced the compact disk. Two years later, when Columbia celebrated Stern's forty years on their label with a ten-year extension of his contract, designation as Artist Laureate, a special logo and a reception at the New York Public Library, the number of his recordings, which included concertos, sonatas, chamber works and the ever-popular petits fours by sixty-two composers, stood a little over two hundred.[25]

In January 1946, Hurok recommended "the 'magnificent' young violinist" to Serge Koussevitzky, the legendary conductor of the Boston Symphony, with the latest Olin Downes review attached. "Incidentally COLUMBIA has just signed him for two concerti, following completion of his featured performance in the forthcoming WARNER BROTHERS film, HUMORESQUE," he added.[26]

The gig in Hollywood was one more leading indicator in what was already an upward trend. A medley of popular tropes about a Lower East Side violin prodigy who leaves his Jewish mother, his childhood sweetheart and a promising career in 1918 to make the world safe for democracy, it first appeared as a magazine story by Fannie Hurst. In 1920, Paramount released it as a silent film.

This time, it appeared in sound—and plenty of it. Zachary Gold, a twenty-eight-year-old screenwriter, and playwright Clifford Odets, a favorite of the prewar left, had meanwhile transformed it into a classic movie weepie about the unrequited love of an Upper East Side playgirl for the Lower East Side prodigy. Joan Crawford and John Garfield signed on as principal characters. What was needed was a prodigious violinist.

It was credibly reported that Heifetz wanted $100,000 and Menuhin $80,000 before Jack Warner, the studio's CEO, lost patience and ordered the film's producer Hal Wallis to find someone else. Stern, who had recently played at the Hollywood Bowl, was conveniently in view and earshot. Dispatched to audition him, the film's composer Franz Waxman declared him entirely fit for the assignment. Stern happily accepted what was reported to be an offer of $20,000–$25,000. As he explained to Potok, he then showed Garfield how to hold a violin so it wouldn't be mistaken for a tennis racket or baseball bat, fiddled the socks off a *Carmen* Fantasy that Waxman composed to show off what he could do, and managed concurrently to fly off to concert engagements thirteen times between scenes.[27]

A "mawkish lamentation on the hopelessness of love," declared Bosley Crowther in his *New York Times* review. It was no exaggeration. Stern went unmentioned, his off-screen participation considered news unfit to print. But Crowther pronounced the music "splendid," Waxman's Fantasy survived to become standard repertory, and Warner Bros. earned almost $4 million on an investment of about $2 million.[28]

Four decades later, inquiries about Stern's role and impressions still trickled into his office. Young people who watched *All the President's Men* ran out and enrolled in journalism schools, a writer from St. Louis reflected. She wondered whether young people who watched *Humoresque* had run out and enrolled in conservatories. Not that he knew of, Stern replied via his secretary.[29]

Over the next decade, with only his hands visible, *Humoresque* allowed him to boldly go where no violinist had gone before. In 1953, *Tonight We Sing*, a dubious biography of Hurok, produced by Twentieth Century–Fox, allowed the chubby five-and-a-half-foot Stern to be seen on screen complete as the supersized six-foot, 220-pound Eugène Ysaÿe.

In 1955, he showed up on Jack Benny's TV show as coconspirator with Benny's long-suffering valet Rochester, in a scheme to persuade Benny, a decent amateur violinist who made a memorable career as a dedicated but hopelessly disastrous one, that he is a great violinist. A year later, he returned to network TV for a guest appearance on Perry Como's variety show. This time the shtick was a pretend violin lesson with Stern as pretend teacher and Como as pretend student. It ends to general hilarity with hundreds of thousand pretend dollars' worth of pretend Guarneri in pieces.

Scriptwriters regularly looked for an opportunity for Stern to be Stern, with Zakin at the ready and Wieniawski conveniently at hand. Encores with Stern as host were usual too. In 1961, Benny was a guest at Carnegie Hall, where he was honored for a lifetime of musical philanthropy and invited to join Stern and the Philadelphia Orchestra in the first movement of the Bach d minor concerto before a delighted audience. In 1980, while on tour in Israel, Como stayed in Stern's apartment as his guest, while Stern, on tour in Paris, played a total of 17 concerts over two months that included 21 solo pieces and 12 concertos with 2 orchestras.

Meanwhile, he went about his business in ever-widening concentric circles. Between 1946 and 1948, he would play 193 concerts, coast-to-coast, border-to-border, across the continental United States, as well as Havana, Honolulu, and the Town Hall of Auckland, New Zealand.

In summer 1948, he left for his first tour of Europe. The itinerary included an austere and grubby postwar Britain, France, Switzerland and Italy, as well as Scandinavia. As he would remember ever after, his appearance in Sweden coincided with the assassination by Jewish terrorists, known colloquially as the Stern Gang, of Count Folke Bernadotte, the Swedish diplomat dispatched by the United Nations to mediate the first Arab-Israeli War.[30]

The tour was remembered as a huge success, though at least one reviewer felt the need to explain that Stern, despite being an American, played with a European soul. Britain was a learning experience. Harold Holt, Britain's closest approximation of a Hurok, acquired him for his Celebrity Concerts series and connected him with the local equivalent of Civic Concerts. Presenters everywhere were unfailingly thoughtful and helpful. But as Hurok reportedly observed, "If people want to stay away, you can't stop them." Edinburgh's Usher Hall seats some 1,800. An audience of 54 showed up there for Stern's local debut.

Yet even Edinburgh turned out to be a winner. He returned to New York as he usually did from anywhere with a network of connections and friendships that would last him for the rest of the century. Among them were Michael Rainer and Ian Hunter, both strong candidates for a Managers Hall of Fame, if only there were one.

Rainer, whose organizational skills might have impressed the coordinator of a moon shot, was heir to a Paris-based family business reaching back to the 1920s. His list included Rudolf Serkin, the Berlin Philharmonic and a troika of the era's leading sopranos—Elisabeth Schwarzkopf, Birgit Nilsson and Joan Sutherland.

Hunter, one of the 54 at Stern's Edinburgh debut, would become director of the Edinburgh Festival and Holt's successor, as well as Stern's go-to man for assignments that might have challenged the inventive Hurok. Who better to coordinate Stern's British schedule with center court tickets for Wimbledon? Who better to take temporary custody of a consignment of Cuban cigars from an Israeli admirer that Stern had rerouted to London when U.S. customs refused to allow delivery in New York?[31] The lesson for both parties was obvious. Artists play for fees and fun. Agents' work is never done.

As a matter of principle, Stern also continued *not* to play in Germany. He preferred to play for audiences he liked, he explained for the next fifty years to interviewers who continued to ask him. Yet he made sure that his protégés played there, maintained cordial relations with German colleagues like the conductor Kurt Masur, and thought the world of Anne-Sophie Mutter.

Soon after returning from his first tour of Europe, he left again for a first tour of Latin America. The year after, he performed for the first time in a newly independent Israel, where audience after audience overflowed the available space. The discovery of Israel transformed his sense of identity, even his life.

Wherever, whenever, the show went on—undeterred by snow, rain, heat, gloom of night and even wartime contingency. In 1997, a fan in Pioneer, California, remembered an evening in 1943 when the local series brought Stern for a concert in Richmond, California. An antiaircraft balloon broke loose, dragged its cable across a power line, and plunged the concert hall into darkness. Stern went on playing.[32] In 1991, when wartime solidarity again brought Stern to Israel, an air alert and threatened Iraqi gas attack interrupted a Mozart concerto in Jerusalem. The orchestra cleared the stage. The audience donned gas masks. Teddy Kollek, the city's redoubtable mayor, marveled at how Stern again resumed playing.[33]

In early March 1946, Stern and Zakin reached Milwaukee in a record snowstorm for what was to be their first local engagement. Coming from the north, the Chicago & Northwestern's 400 arrived a little after 8 P.M., concert time. But there was no car or cab in sight. Anna Robinson, secretary of the Civic Concert association, had sold 2,300 advance tickets. She found a volunteer to pick up the artists at the station.

Dispensing with the usual concert dress, Stern appeared onstage a little after nine, "and played that fiddle for all he, and it, were worth," for an audience of 150, the *Milwaukee Journal*'s Walter Monfried reported. As in New York, the program included some solo Bach, Wieniawski's second violin concerto and the Brahms d minor sonata, a Bartok rhapsody, still a shocker at the time, as well as Saint-Saëns's indestructible Introduction and Rondo Capriccioso. "A superb violinist," Stern had even announced program changes "in clear and understandable English," Monfried noted. He hoped that "this young Mr. Stern" would come back on a happier day.

Like the Brahms sonata, unflappable, show-must-go-on dedication was still prominent in his repertory a couple of decades later when Stern and Zakin realized that their airline had lost their luggage and music en route to Schenectady. This time a patient audience waited two hours for them to appear, again in street dress. Meanwhile, they hunted for material enough "to piece together a passable concert" among the resources of the local library. "It was not bad considering what had happened," it was recalled.[34]

On his return to Carnegie in March 1946, Stern had replaced his Guadagnini with his first Guarneri del Gesù, acquired for $65,000, the equivalent of some $620,000 by the time he died. He was clearly doing something right. A year later, he joined Leonard Bernstein, his senior by two years and at least as prodigious as himself, for a performance of Prokofiev's First Violin Concerto in Rochester, New York. They were called back to repeat the second movement scherzo. "Isn't it wonderful to be young and famous?" Bernstein asked as they acknowledged salvos of applause. The answer was obvious.

His friendship with Bernstein would continue till Bernstein's death in 1990. He fondly remembered an evening in Venice in 1954, where they had come to premiere the Serenade, Bernstein's violin concerto, with the Israel Philharmonic, and afterward had gone to dinner. Like the rabbis in the Passover Haggadah, who talked about the exodus from Egypt till their students reminded them it was time for morning prayers, they then talked till sunrise "about life, about what each of us was looking for, about what we believed in." But acknowledged or otherwise, the subtext was Wordsworth, updated for a pair of spectacularly gifted American Jews. "Bliss was it in that dawn to be alive, but to be young was very heaven."

Thinking back, Stern could recall only one personal experience with anti-Semitism, when he and his family were turned away by a hotel in upstate New York.[35] Still in their thirties, he and Bernstein now found themselves honored guests in the city that inspired Shylock, invented the ghetto, and even gave the ghetto its name.

Like the Venetians, he had also discovered the East, though the route that took him there would not have occurred to Marco Polo. His introduction to Britain a few years earlier had been somewhat tentative. This time, as he happily reported in a long letter to "Dear Miss Lutie," a reprise in late 1952 was so successful that he expected to return the following year for more concerts in London, as well as four or five at the Edinburgh Festival. After that came Japan and India.

With commercial jet travel still in its infancy, a trip from Honolulu to Tokyo meant eighteen hours, twelve of them in flight, he informed Walter Prude of the Hurok office on two pages of hand-typed, single-spaced Imperial Hotel stationery. The international date line added much of a new day on arrival. A grandiose airport reception, with flower girls, a delegation from NHK, Japan's public broadcasting company, plus interviews, photo ops, business conversations and dinner, added still more to what he calculated to be a twenty-three-hour day.

The following week he played five concerts in 90-degree heat with humidity to match in a city where air conditioning too was still over the horizon. "In desperation we had white jackets made because it became unbearable to play in full dress," he added. His instruments also suffered, and a Guarneri came unglued. But the size and enthusiasm of local audiences exceeded even the weather and the overwhelming hospitality. Though time constraints put a side visit to Korea out of reach, he found time to play at American military hospitals in Japan.

Meanwhile, he was taken to see everything and meet everyone short of the emperor. He even had an interesting conversation "about politics, culture, music, economics, etc." with the Speaker of the Diet on a train from Tokyo to Osaka. He assumed on arrival that the crowd at the station had come to meet the Speaker. He only then realized that it had come to meet him.

What impressed him especially, in a country where he couldn't speak easily or read at all, was the sense of living in a bubble. Usable photos and translated reviews were slow to come. But the message from Nippon Columbia, at least, came through loud and clear. His LPs had been doing well in Japan for a couple of years at $9–$10 each. The royalties had been transferred to New York. But the company would be happy to prepare a statement for him while he was in Japan, they informed him. "Which I, of course, will not refuse to look at!" he reported to another Hurok staffer.

A few weeks later, en route from Manila to Calcutta, he wrote his friend Martin Feinstein that there was more to the story than he had realized. Five weeks after he'd played in Japan, four reviews had finally shown up in translation. All were outstandingly hostile. Their animus was part anti-American, part anti-NHK, animated by a feeling that the broadcaster favored foreign over local talent. A third source, he inferred, was culture lag on the part of aging reviewers, whose reflexes were stuck in a prewar time warp with Alfred Cortot, Jacques Thibaud and Efrem Zimbalist.[36] Luckily, he estimated, up to 80 percent of his audiences were thirty-five or under. It was an audience that would remain loyal to the end.

His passage to India, where Western music was as foreign as baseball, could hardly have been more different. His host, Victor Paranjoti, a onetime government official, cement company executive, and business journalist, was also president of the Bombay Madrigal Singers' Organisation. This was where Stern came in. Founded only six years before, the host organization was "run by young people—students, stenographers and so on mostly—people whose deep love for music made them take up music-making and the running of concerts when older and wealthier folks threw in the sponge," Paranjoti explained.[37] Stern and Zakin agreed to play for travel expenses. Their unspent per diem went to the society's piano fund.

With time off for the Taj Mahal, they played three concerts—Bombay, New Delhi and Calcutta—in four days. Thanks to

Paranjoti, they enjoyed a language they could understand, full houses and enthusiastic audiences, including Stern's protégé-to-be, Zubin Mehta, age eleven,[38] who would grow up to play with him as conductor of the Israel Philharmonic. But it would be their only passage to India. As a reward for trimming their fee, they were taken to meet Prime Minister Jawaharlal Nehru, who clearly wished he were somewhere else until Stern got his attention with a question about misery like none he had ever encountered.

An inadvertent bit of damage to his violin also led Stern to Parshos Ratnagar, a trustee of Bombay's Prince of Wales Museum, and most probably the only Stradivarius owner in India. Ratnagar volunteered first aid. On his return to New York, Stern naturally took his instrument to the legendary Simone Fernando Sacconi for summit-level attention. Sacconi, according to Stern, was volubly distressed by Ratnagar's improvisation. But as so often, the friendship survived. Some years later, Ratnagar was allowed to take his violinist granddaughter, Maya Magub, to play for Stern at Claridge's Hotel in London. She would grow up to be a studio and chamber player in Hollywood.[39]

IN 1961 HE RETURNED to Australia for eight weeks, twenty-seven concerts and a fortuitous meeting with a young and formidably gifted pianist, whose lapse into adolescent schizoaffective disorder was later the subject of the movie *Shine*.[40] The 1971 visit to Australia was already his fourth.

But his most consequential encounter took place in a tiny corner of Europe, ceded to France by Spain just short of three hundred years earlier. Once again, time and place coincided with good fortune.

The late 1930s had brought the Budapest Quartet to Mills College in Oakland, across the bay from San Francisco. Stern's teacher, Blinder, a friend and contemporary of the quartet's first violinist, brought Stern to meet the quartet. A tennis date with Alexander Schneider, the quartet's second violinist and his senior by eight years, led to their lifetime friendship.

In 1947, while preparing for a European tour, Schneider worked in New York with the cellist Diran Alexandrian, an old associate and colleague of the legendary cellist Pablo Casals. Alexandrian proposed that Schneider play for Casals while in Europe. He even volunteered a letter of introduction.

In semiretirement and voluntary exile since 1939, when the Spanish Civil War ended with the victory of Francisco Franco's Nationalists, Casals now lived in two upstairs rooms in Prades, a village on the French edge of the Pyrenees, with a four-digit population, many of them fellow refugees. He rarely played in public. He also refused to play in any country that recognized Franco. But his reply to Alexandrian was quick and affirmative.

Three days with Casals sufficed to persuade Schneider that he wanted more, wanted to play chamber music, and wanted to bring friends. In Fall 1948 he began intensive study of the Bach solo sonatas and partitas, which he would play complete in concert, still something of a novelty, and record complete on LP, still another novelty. As he had promised himself, he also returned to Prades, this time with friends. A disappointment but no surprise, Casals was unwilling to play in the United States, which recognized Franco. But he did agree to a concert in Prades in 1950, the bicentennial of Bach's death.

On his return to the States, Schneider assembled a high-octane steering committee, beginning with the patrons Elizabeth Sprague Coolidge and Rosalie "Winnie" Leventritt. Olin Downes of the *New York Times* was co-opted to make the festival news fit to print. *Life* magazine photographers Gjon Mili and Margaret Bourke-White were invited to make sure the festival was seen as well as heard; the record executives David Oppenheim and Goddard Lieberson, to assure that it would be heard globally after it was over.

But high-octane players were the most necessary of the necessary conditions. This was where Stern came in, as did an orchestra of thirty-three; twenty of them Americans, and four were solo violinists, including the Hungarians Joseph Szigeti and Stefi Geyer, as well as Stern and Schneider. Stern recalled in his memoir that Schneider called a year ahead and virtually ordered him to play at the festival. As Stern recalled it, he was delighted. As Schneider recalled it, Stern, "who is now the most generous artist I know," tried to set conditions. He only wanted to come if he could play in a trio with Casals and Dame Myra Hess.

It didn't happen. But he came anyway, as did an audience that included the French president, the Belgian queen, Prince Rainier of Monaco, Baron Rothschild, the Princesse de Polignac, a descendant of the Singer sewing machine fortune, who thought to bring along a case of Pommery champagne, and the young Jacqueline Bouvier, who would marry John F. Kennedy in 1953.[41] A year later the festival decamped for one year only to the comparatively metropolitan Perpignan, with its population of 80,000. In 1952 it returned to Prades.

Be it for its effect on the host or on the guests, the rediscovery of Casals was catalytic, leaving no one unmoved. "It was you, Sasha, who took pity on my silence," Casals told Schneider. "Your career is that which you deserve, and it is a great comfort to me to think of how you respect and care for the gift that you received from God," he wrote Stern on festival letterhead in the afterglow of 1952. "He opened the gates to his garden and his heart and I discovered colors and sonorities there that I had never imagined," Stern told a French interviewer some thirty-five years later.[42]

Decades later, the festival's long shadow could still be seen from Prades and Perpignan, where the festivals began, to Puerto Rico, where they resumed after Casals resettled there in 1956. They continued there until his death in 1973. "We should be grateful if you would write to us your message or essay," a Japanese editor requested of Stern in 1987 when Casals Hall, a chamber music hall with 511 seats, opened in Tokyo." Stern replied in 482 words, beginning, "No one has ever come away from having met and known Pablo Casals without undergoing a profound change in his or her thinking of how to make music." Thirteen years later, when asked by the *New York Times* what he would take along to the proverbial desert island, he included Casals's recordings of the Bach cello suites and the Marlboro Festival recordings of the Brandenburg Concertos, as well as his fiddle, cigars and wife.[43]

Meanwhile, Prades lived on in a piano trio born there in 1950. Stern, still under thirty, and the pianist Eugene Istomin, twenty-five, so liked what they heard of one another that they decided to look for a cellist. Leonard Rose, thirty-two, had been principal of both the Cleveland Orchestra and the New York Philharmonic at a precocious age. He and Stern had been friends since the 1940s. Their 1954 recording of the Brahms concerto for violin and cello with Bruno Walter had won a Grand Prix du Disque. He had recently embarked on a solo career. He seemed an optimal fit.

Though uncommon, the idea was not entirely a novelty. Between 1906 and the early 1930s, Casals himself had played and recorded in a celebrated trio with the pianist Alfred Cortot and the violinist Jacques Thibaud, both like himself A-list soloists with their own careers. Before the premature death of their cellist Emanuel Feuermann in 1941, the pianist Artur Rubinstein and violinist Jascha Heifetz had played together too. In 1949, with Gregor Piatigorsky as cellist, they agreed to a legendary four-concert series at Chicago's Ravinia Park, the summer home of the Chicago Symphony. Known immediately and ever after as the Million Dollar Trio, they also recorded their repertory for RCA Victor as well as posterity.

It was not a marriage made in heaven. Though the listener would never know it from hearing them, they reportedly interacted like bull elephants in musth. The issue was which of three superstar names and supersized egos should appear first on the record jacket. Since the genre was piano trio by definition, the pianist should logically come first, Rubinstein argued. There were also trios in which the pianist was the subordinate, Heifetz replied. An unidentified executive at RCA finessed the difference. Heifetz and Rubinstein appeared on the top line, side by side. They also never played together again.

None of them diffident by nature, Istomin, Stern and Rose also had their differences. But billing was not one of them. Taking his cue from their common gender, James Wade, an American in Korea, suggested SIR Trio as an option. IRS Trio, a reminder of their tax status, was another possibility.[44] With the Million Dollar Trio inevitably prominent in their field of vision, and tongues firmly in cheek, the players themselves proposed the $683,926.50 Trio.[45] While preparing a cover story some years later, the *Saturday Review* found a pragmatic alternative. "Three Men on a Hobby."

By this time, the opportunity and challenges of playing for profit had long since superseded the joys of playing for fun. Like their emblematic predecessors in 1949, they made their premiere appearance at Ravinia before an outdoor audience of 3,400 and in near-100 percent relative humidity. Reviewers were skeptical that three alpha soloists could learn to play well together. But so were the players. "At the beginning, we envisaged the thing as an idealized fraternity," Istomin told an interviewer. But it wasn't. "We are three major personalities, three egos, three prima donnas," said Rose.

Schneider, in an antic moment, dispatched a postcard reproduction of Goya's *Fight with Cudgels* (*Duelo a Garrotazos*) from the Prado. Two men, knee-deep in mud, are whaling away at one another with clubs. "Beethoven sonatas, Perfect Coordination by Isaac Stern, Eugene Istomin, Painted especially for Col.[umbia] Records by Fr. Goya," read the message—in red ink.[46]

The addition of a third player increased the permutations for conflict from one to four. "We have to blend and give in and come to a common understanding," said Rose.[47] A cooling-off period seemed indicated.

Six years later, at the first Israel Festival, they again performed outdoors, this time in the ancient Roman amphitheater at Caesarea. "It was on this first tour of Israel that Eugene and Rose, both believers in arriving early and in diligent preconcert preparation, found that Stern had the alarming habit of showing up at the last minute and going onstage cold," Istomin's biographer noted.[48] Medical intervention was also needed to relieve a pinched nerve that almost incapacitated Rose's left hand. And yet, as Galileo famously said, it moved. "We rehearsed like hell and tore everything to pieces," Rose remembered. "We got glowing reviews and it was really the start."[49]

A year later, and just weeks after the Bay of Pigs, the CIA's abortive invasion of Cuba, what had begun as Alexander Schneider's quest for authentic Bach and rediscovery of Casals led to Camelot at 1600 Pennsylvania Avenue, Washington, D.C., 20500. In November 1961, Casals himself had appeared at the White House with Schneider and the pianist Mieczysław Horszowski to perform for Luis Muñoz-Marín, Puerto Rico's first elected governor. This time, May 11, 1962, the occasion was dinner at the White House for 166, including André Malraux, France's minister of culture, who was one of the era's intellectual superstars, and a walking anthology of American arts and letters.

The menu included lobster en Bellevue, stuffed bar Polignac and potatoes Parisienne. Istomin, Stern and Rose added the

Schubert B-flat Trio, D. 898. Istomin looked on appalled as Stern mixed cheerfully with the guests. President John F. Kennedy, clearly in over his head, thanked Stern "and his two accompanists." Discreetly corrected, he invited the trio upstairs to the family quarters for a drink and a companionable chat.

The White House led in turn to multiple tours of Europe and Latin America as well as the Philadelphia Orchestra's pension fund and multiple full houses at Carnegie Hall, a commemoration of the United Nations' twentieth anniversary, the Casals Festival in 1970, a Beethoven marathon in the bicentennial year of the composer's birth, and recordings of most of the standard trio literature. Booked in Fort Wayne, Indiana, while in Chicago for a four-concert series, they remembered only while en route that, unlike Chicago, Fort Wayne is in the Eastern Zone. They arrived at the concert hall an hour late. No one had left.

Rumors of impending implosion were never far behind. But, like the proverbial report of Mark Twain's death, they remained an exaggeration. On the contrary, the band played on without interruption until Rose's death in 1984. But for the leukemia that killed him, it might well have played on indefinitely. Stern and Istomin soldiered on without him to a final recital in 1997. From there to the end, Stern continued with friends and protégés. Columbia, which had marketed Stern, Casals, Schneider, Rose, Istomin et al. for decades on LP, now marketed Stern, Yo-Yo Ma, Jaime Laredo, Cho-Liang Lin, Sharon Robinson, Michael Tree, Emanuel Ax et al. on CDs that could still be heard and even seen decades later thanks to two more innovations: YouTube and the DVD.

Noteworthy, though hardly noted, was a back-to-the-future dimension that reconnected Stern's career and legacy with their historical roots. Like Joachim a century earlier, he had made his way from the social periphery to the era's Big Apple, from the peaks of virtuosity to the profundities of chamber music, from working musician to civic monument, and from adolescent promise to a prominent obituary in the *New York Times*.

Like Joachim, he had extended the parameters of a guild whose members, still dressed for the Congress of Berlin in the age of Brooks Brothers and L.L. Bean, were ordinarily seen only in front of a piano or to a conductor's left. Again like Joachim, he extended—or at least tried—to extend the parameters of a literature that seemingly ended with Richard, if not of Johann, Strauss.

His regard for the music of his time already set him apart from some of his most prominent peers. On tour in Italy in 1952, he was underwhelmed by a visit to composer Luigi Dallapiccola. But a year later, as he reported in a long, chatty letter to the conductor Igor Markevitch, he discovered, and was bowled over, by the Bartók violin concerto, a twentieth-century masterpiece that later turned out to be the composer's second of two.[50] Twenty years later, he would add the first concerto at the request of its dedicatee Stefi Geyer, who also happened to be the wife of Walter Schulthess, Stern's Swiss manager.[51] He would meanwhile go on to play and record concertos by Samuel Barber, Sergei Prokofiev, Igor Stravinsky, and Alban Berg. None of them were personal acquaintances, let alone friends. But all of them were as real and present in his world as Brahms, Schumann and Mendelssohn had been in Joachim's, and if several were no longer alive, they had at least been alive in living memory.

It was 1964 before he performed and recorded Paul Hindemith's concerto of 1939 with Bernstein. He regarded it as one of the century's two or three best, and berated himself for not performing and recording it until half a year after the composer's death. He was amazed that it wasn't in everybody's repertory, he told the composer's wife in a condolence note.[52] The question was still worth asking a couple of decades after his own death, thirty-eight years after Hindemith's.

Bartók was a particular favorite. Stern considered his second sonata the greatest piece for violin and piano since the d minor sonata that was Brahms's third.[53] His enthusiasm dated back to his teenage years in San Francisco when the Budapest Quartet introduced him to the Bartók quartets at Mills College. In 1953 he played the Bartók concerto at Carnegie Hall, where he had played Szymanowski ten years earlier. In 1958, he recorded it with Bernstein. In 1967, Eugene Ormandy, the veteran conductor of the Philadelphia Orchestra, who wanted Stern to know that he rarely wrote fan letters, wrote him a fan letter. He was preparing a performance of the concerto with another player. A friend had loaned him the Stern/Bernstein recording for reference. He wanted Stern to know that "you have superseded anything I have heard you play, and this means a great deal from one who has conducted for you countless times."[54]

A Main Line Philadelphian who attended a recital in 1983 was unpersuaded, even incensed, when Stern paired Bartók's first sonata with Mozart's K. 301 in the first half of a program that continued with Schumann and Beethoven. He had learned from his third-grade teacher that music comprises harmony, rhythm and melody, the writer declared. "I'll concede harmony and rhythm, but if you can hum, whistle, sing or play a 5 bar piece of melody, I'll listen to the whole piece ten times in a row."

It took Stern nearly two years to respond. But not surprisingly, he was unmoved by the argument. "We neither live, dress, eat, sleep or travel in the style of the eighteenth or nineteenth century," he replied firmly. "As performers we are conscious of that and pick the best of each period to make the music our own and present it to our listeners." Any professional musician could hum or whistle Bartók, he added.[55]

There was a lifetime of premieres to support his point. The genesis of the first, in 1950, might well have inspired a novel or movie. In 1946, William Schuman, then president of Juilliard and first Pulitzer Prize winner for composition three years earlier, began work on a violin concerto. In principle, it was good to go in 1947 with Koussevitzky, the Boston Symphony and Samuel Dushkin, who commissioned it, as soloist. But unfortunately for Dushkin, neither Schuman nor Koussevitzky thought he was up to the challenge of playing it. Meanwhile, unfortunately for Schuman, Dushkin had three years of exclusive rights to the score. It was 1950 before Stern, who was Koussevitzky's candidate for the solo, could premiere a first version, and in 1956 a revised second. It was 1959 before the score finally came to rest in published form.[56]

By comparison, the genesis of the next premiere, Bernstein's Serenade, a five-movement concerto allusively based on Plato's

*Symposium*, was the love feast of its subtext. It was also probably as close as both player and composer would get to the respective roles of Joachim and Brahms. "It looks as though it will be difficult for the orchestra," Bernstein noted in July 1954 in a midsummer progress report. "(Like all my pieces, they sound like a breeze but are hell to perform.)" On the eve of the premiere in Venice a few months later, there was a preemptive whistle in the dark. "Isaac, my Isaac," the composer wrote, "whatever happens tonight, fair or foul or flop, I want you to know how much I will always cherish your work on the Serenade." He was still aglow on his return to New York in early October.

"I still get a deep kick when I recall how you played the Serenade," Bernstein told Stern. "You made me love the piece even more than is usual for a composer." Stern was appreciative, with qualifications. "Having been so close to the 'birth' of this work, I would really like to see it through all the way," he reminded Bernstein. "Don't you agree? Hmmm?"[57]

It was 1973 before Stern's first-responder services were again requested, this time by the Pittsburgh Symphony and its conductor William Steinberg, who wanted Stern for a new concerto by George Rochberg. A music professor at the University of Pennsylvania, Rochberg had been a leading serialist until the death of his teenage son in 1964 persuaded him that modernism was "a postage-stamp-sized space to stand on."[58] Stern was amenable. "Let me say in advance," he told Rochberg, "you should have no fears of having any suggestions of how to write or what form it should take."

Two years later, the concerto was enthusiastically received.

"The greatest experience of my musical life," Rochberg called it in a 1 A.M. journal entry, just hours after the premiere. "If it is as good a work as I hope, I think it would be in the interest of everyone concerned to give it as many performances as possible," Stern told Georg Solti, the conductor of the Chicago Symphony. He meant it too, performing it himself some forty-seven times between the premiere in 1975 and 1977. But he also demanded that Rochberg cut it down from the original fifty-one minutes to thirty-seven.

In the years that followed, Stern added no fewer than three more premieres. The first, as elaborately planned as the kickoff to an election campaign, was a multiperformance commitment to the first violin concerto by Krzysztof Penderecki in 1977. Easy to admire, though difficult to whistle, Penderecki was a cultural representative of Polish resistance to Soviet domination years before Lech Walesa had been heard of outside the Gdansk shipyard. The concerto, associated discreetly with his dying father and written for Stern, was a recent change of course, an alternative act of resistance, like Rochberg's, to the mid-century's modernist police.

With three weeks to go to the premiere in Basel, Stern recalled, the final pages were still under negotiation. He was already looking at the fifth version, the composer informed him. "Would you like to try for number six?" Stern asked.[59] He evidently liked what he got. "One of the few important works written for the violin in this century," he declared in an undated program note.

Penderecki seemed happy with it too. Ten years later he approached Stern about a follow-up collaboration. The Spanish court owned a unique set of decorated Strads. The Queen of

Spain had asked Penderecki for a quintet to commemorate the two-hundredth anniversary of their acquisition. He wondered if Stern could get "Rostropovich, Pinky [Zukerman], Shlomo [Mintz], and Yo-Yo [Ma] or Matt [Haimovitz]," together to play it with him.[60] But nothing seems to have come of the project.

The last two premieres, in November 1985 and June 1986 respectively, were mature works in every sense. It was remarkable enough to take on two large, new and difficult pieces in little more than half a year. It was still more remarkable to take them on at or past what most countries consider their statutory retirement age.

The composers were not young, either. Henri Dutilleux was already seventy. Peter Maxwell Davies, at fifty, was young only by comparison. Each was an established figure. Each had been awarded his country's highest honor, the Grand Cross of the Legion of Honor in Dutilleux's case, Companion of Honour in Maxwell Davies's. Each swam purposely and intentionally against the stream of postwar musical orthodoxy. Each felt a concurrent urge to write a violin concerto.

Save for this, they had little in common. Dutilleux, unassuming, unideological, and eminently approachable, lived comfortably but unpretentiously on the Île St. Louis, one of Paris's most desirable neighborhoods. Maxwell Davies, a lifetime contrarian and workaholic, with a soft spot for the music of the Middle Ages and Renaissance, lived without electricity and running water on an Orkney island, where he had been known to work sixteen-hour days.

An unconventional seven-section sequence of four movements

separated by three interludes, Dutilleux's concerto was commissioned by Radio France. But it was dedicated to Stern, the only personal dedication among his six premieres. Its subtitle, *L'Arbre des Songes* (*Tree of Dreams*), while not directly programmatic, was as least associative as the musical material developed like leaves and branches, and the respective movements followed one another like the seasons.

The instrumentation, including an oboe d'amore, piccolo clarinet, five timpani, two suspended cymbals, two tam-tams, crotales, tubular bells, glockenspiel, vibraphone, three bongos, three snare drums, cymbalum, celesta, piano and harp, was as rich in color—and incidental expense—as any Monet. Then came the score itself, which not only called for a virtuoso conductor and virtuoso orchestra in addition to the virtuoso soloist, but required six to seven rehearsals, compared with the usual two to four. If there was an economy, it came, ironically, in Dutilleux's commission, 20,000 francs or 5,000 1984 dollars, according to Stern.

But it was clear from the beginning that Radio France got its money's worth and the piece got the attention it deserved. Stern recorded it soon after its Paris premiere. He then showed it off in Boston, New York, Baltimore, on tour with the Baltimore Symphony, and Montreal, where only a call to Chicago from an understanding airline captain in Denver allowed him to catch the connecting flight that got him to a crucial rehearsal.

A half-generation later he would note like a proud papa that the piece, "which I think is one of the great works of our time," was making its way into the repertory.[61] A quarter-century later, six full performances on YouTube had attracted over 82,000 hits; Leonidas Kavakos, who could have been Stern's son, talked at eloquent length about the piece in a twenty-seven-minute interview with the principal bass player of the Berlin Philharmonic; and Augustin Hadelich, who might have been Stern's grandson, won a Grammy award for his performance of the concerto with the Seattle Symphony.

In June 1986, Maxwell Davies's concerto made its debut in Kirkwall, the largest town and capital of Orkney. With a population just short of five figures, it was one of the unlikeliest venues in music history. The occasion was a double anniversary, the fortieth of the Royal Philharmonic, which commissioned the piece, as well as the tenth of the composer's local St. Magnus Festival.

Sponsor and patron was the Scottish Postal Board, "everybody's dream of what a sponsor should be," the composer noted with good reason. The Board had already advanced £8,000 (about $11,700) before the festival even began. By the time Stern and the orchestra arrived from London, the bill was likely to reach or exceed £15,000. The BBC had also done its bit, dispatching a crew of forty and deploying a satellite link to produce a live broadcast.

Gestation, in fact, went back to 1982 when Ian Hunter, Stern's U.K. manager, proposed the commission, and Maxwell Davies's manager arranged a meeting of presumptive composer and presumptive soloist at Claridge's, London's flagship hotel and Stern's favorite. The blind date led to friendship, multiple editorial conferences and piano tryouts with André Previn, then conductor of the Royal Philharmonic and yet another Friend of Isaac. At the premiere, Stern sensed the landscape of rocks, sea and birds in the character of the piece. The Orkney debut led to London, and from there, like its predecessors, to the recording studio, where the composer personally engaged in the editing process to the point of splicing individual notes.

Donal Henahan of the *New York Times*, reviewing the American premiere in 1988, respected the piece, but didn't really like it.[62] "I believe that it is a work that will continue into decades to become a standard work performed by many colleagues who appreciate both challenge and beauty in the works they choose to play," Stern wrote in what looks like a program note in 1993.[63]

Henahan also considered it newsworthy that the novelty, as was usual with contemporary pieces, had been programmed with the familiar, in this case Mozart's Third Concerto in G major, and that a memory lapse had caused Stern to stop the orchestra, apologize to the audience, then resume from the beginning. It was a year of 60 concerts and 200,000 miles of travel, Stern would later note in his memoir, and "there were, of course, other things as well."[64]

"As you will remember, I told you that I am going to travel only 6 months of the year and only accept those concerts that I know will give me musical pleasure, rather than taking blindly a fully-booked tour without examination," he told his Swiss manager Émile Rossier in January 1968. "Of course, it has taken a little time to convince all my managers that this is the way I want it."

In February, Rossier dutifully informed "dear friends" that Stern would play in Switzerland before leaving on a Tuesday to see President Johnson. He would then return to Europe the following Sunday for a concert in Florence. The more he did, the better he felt, Stern replied when Rossier suggested he might like to take things a little easier. He may even have meant it. Rossier liked the answer, but it made him a little uneasy, he conceded. He would not be surprised if Stern were to "tell him tomorrow" that he was tired and needed to relax. In April, Stern informed Rossier that he had lost thirty pounds, with another ten to go, and had also stopped smoking.[65] He may have meant that too.

A few weeks later, he learned officially that he was urgently needed in Dubrovnik. "It is only the great importance which the American embassy and especially Ambassador Elbrick attach to the Festival and the opportunity it provides for enhancing the prestige of American cultural achievements that encourage me to write you at this very late date," the cultural attaché informed him. Though unavailable himself, Stern proposed Rose, the pianist Mischa Dichter and the LaSalle Quartet as pinch hitters.[66] But he made it to Dubrovnik a year later. He was also received by Marshal Tito.

A story, popular in Bonn in the early 1970s, features Horst Ehmke, chief of staff to the Federal Republic's then Chancellor and Nobel laureate Willy Brandt. Formidably bright, energetic and self-assured in equal parts, Ehmke is seen bounding out of the Federal Chancellery into the first limousine at the door. "Where to?" asks the driver. "It doesn't matter," says Ehmke. "I'm needed everywhere."

With minimal adjustments, the story could have been told with the same wry admiration about Isaac Stern. It didn't come cheap, as an otherwise admiring fan observed in a review of

Stern's memoir. His first child was born while he was in the Soviet Union. He left for Latin America a few days after his return to the United States. He was away again when his second child arrived. But concert tours, unlike babies, were booked years in advance, and *Pacta sunt servanda* (Agreements must be kept) had been part of his job description since at least that long-ago winter when he arrived in Milwaukee to play for 150 people in the midst of a record snowstorm.[67]

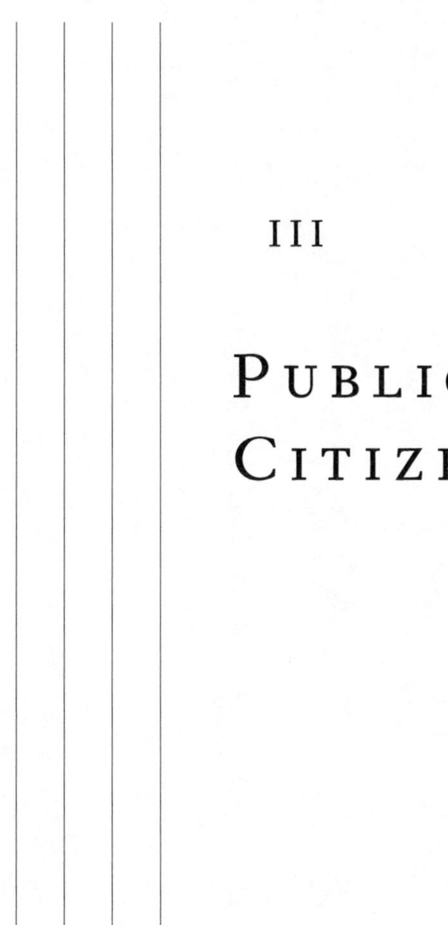

III

# Public Citizen

"SOME ARE BORN GREAT, SOME ACHIEVE GREATNESS, and some have greatness thrust upon them," a slightly confused Malvolio notes in Act III of Shakespeare's *Twelfth Night*. Had he substituted public citizenship for greatness, he could have said the same of Isaac Stern. It was unlikely that a basically apolitical immigrant kid, practicing the violin in San Francisco, would be born to public citizenship, though given Stern's basic temperament and a different time and place, it was certainly imaginable that he might one day achieve it. But for any American male who came of age on or after December 7, 1941, Admiral Yamamoto's fateful decision to attack Pearl Harbor settled the matter. For the better part of the next four years, even a rookie virtuoso with flat feet, a pilonidal sinus and a 4-F classification from his draft board could hardly help but have public citizenship in one form or another thrust upon him.

In time, Stern would discover that he not only liked public citizenship. He also had an uncommon gift for it. But like his taste and affinity for the violin, his taste and affinity for civic activism came unannounced, even serendipitously. While in Chicago in 1943, he was improbably co-opted as an accessory to the Manhattan Project. As in San Francisco years before, there was even a friend who played an inadvertent role in his self-discovery.

In early 1942, Arthur Compton, the 1927 Nobel laureate in physics, established the Metallurgical Laboratory at the University of Chicago to study the properties and practical potential of plutonium. Within a year or so, the staff would grow to over 2,000. Among them was Hy Goldsmith, Stern's former New York apartment mate, as the project's director of information. Stern had even helped with the job application. He now stayed with Goldsmith as he had in New York, and played recreationally with and for Goldsmith's friends and colleagues.

In December 1942, Metallurgical Lab personnel set up the world's first self-sustaining artificial chain reaction in a squash court under the stands of Stagg Field, the university's dormant football stadium. Some months later, when Stern was again in town to play with the Chicago Symphony, it occurred to Goldsmith and his colleagues that he was exceptionally well qualified to be the lab animal in their next experiment.

"Since we were working for the Army and Navy Air Corps at the time, security plus the nature of the experiment made it impossible for us to tell you very much or very accurately about what we were doing," a member of the research team explained years later while proposing that he and Stern meet for dinner in New York. But it was clear enough in retrospect that development of a user-friendly cockpit that allowed a pilot to bail out safely in the event of emergency was the point of the exercise.

To test the effect of oxygen deprivation on mental and physical performance, Stern was sealed in a decompression chamber and told to play at simulated altitudes from sea level to 18,000 feet. Meanwhile, instruments whirred, film rolled and his performance of the final, presto, movement from Bach's g minor solo sonata was recorded.

"Under these circumstances, you appeared quite cyanotic (anoxic)," Stern learned. It was another way of saying that oxygen deprivation had turned him blue. He had also been "quite euphoric ('high' as from scotch) and somewhat hyperactive." Yet remarkably, his playing was as perfect at oxygen-deprived 18,000 feet as it was at sea level. Similar experiments performed on the university rifle and tennis teams produced similar results and similar reassurance to fighter pilots that they could do what was needed if worst came to worst.

"Our observations obtained on you are probably the only ones of their kind which have ever been obtained," his correspondent added. "They were of timely interest to the war effort, to science and—who knows, to history."[1]

But Chicago was still only virtual reality. The draft classification, when it finally arrived in October 1943, was the real thing. He had already performed at military bases and Stage Door Canteens in such metropolitan centers as New York, Philadelphia and San Francisco. Disqualified for military service, he was nonetheless determined to do what he could.

"Everybody was out there doing something," he explained to Potok. "I couldn't just go on playing the fiddle, making a career." At this point, his thoughts turned to the much-adapted medieval story of the juggler who honors the Virgin Mary with the talent that is his only asset. If he couldn't serve with the troops, Stern reasoned, he could at least play for them and organize colleagues to do the same.[2]

The United Service Organizations (USO), created on the eve of the war as a federation of charitable support groups, needed only to be persuaded that it was the logical sponsor of a troupe of entertainers like none they'd ever seen. This done, wheels turned.

Designated Unit #264, a gang of five—Zakin as well as Stern, Frederick Jagel, a Metropolitan Opera tenor who had sung 34 roles in 23 seasons, Polyna Stoska, a Met soprano, who like Stern recorded for Columbia, and Robert Weede, a respected Met baritone, who would go on to a second career on Broadway—appeared for induction. They were issued green uniforms, prophylactically commissioned captain in the event that they were taken prisoner, and vaccinated against such bugs as might be awaiting them by the same doctor who had attended to Stern's surgical recuperation. They then left for Guadalcanal and New Caledonia via Hawaii and Guam.

Over the next seven weeks, Stern reported in his memoir, they flew 20,000 miles and played 61 concerts for an estimated 140,000 listeners. Over six weeks, playing wherever he was taken during the day, and returning at night, Stern shared a small beachfront tent on Guadalcanal with a young radiologist named Robert Warner.

It was the kind of relationship, Warner recalled, where "you are either very good friends or you never want to see one another again." Happily, it was the former. Stern reported at length to Warner's mother and wife on his return to the United States, and there were postwar reunions afterward whenever he was anywhere near Buffalo.[3]

Appreciative reminiscences over the next half-century confirmed that he had made an impression. About the last thing his "raggedy bunch of combat Marines" had in mind, a former platoon commander remembered, was a clutch of concert performers. But they taught him a lesson. "It became very clear that excellence is something that can be recognized by everyone . . . , and the thunderous applause brought you back for encore after encore."[4]

A Navy veteran who had doubled on piano accordion at an engine overhaul base in New Caledonia remembered fondly how Stern had invited him to join in duet versions of "Under the Double Eagle," "Ciribiribin" and "Over the Waves." He had always "cherished the event," he said, and this was surely true.[5]

A year later, Stern had occasion to recycle the lessons of Guadalcanal in Iceland and Greenland, a very different but equally improbable venue forty-seven miles inside the Arctic Circle, playing for audiences as small as ten. In the meantime, he and Zakin played some fifty concerts between Houston and Quebec, the Allies won the war in Europe, and Stern, like millions of other Americans, searched for compass points in the evolving postwar landscape.

His USO experience taught him two lessons, he explained in years to come. The first was practical. Anyone can succeed, he told a German interviewer, if he knows his business and approaches his audience without condescension. His own approach favored a simple and familiar opener like Stephen Foster. Once he'd established a connection, he could play whatever he wanted, including solo Bach.[6]

The other lesson was civic. "If you're alive and sentient to what is going on, you have to know how that life affects yours and what is going on in the body politic that affects your private life and your private concerns," he told Potok. "You can't divorce yourself from the world."

Over the next half-century, it became ever more apparent that the second lesson was especially close to his heart. Within a couple of years, it would lead to an experience that told relatively little not already known about himself, but a good deal about the evolving postwar era.

In March 1949, the National Council of the Arts, Sciences and Professions, a front organization of the Communist Party USA, convened the Scientific and Cultural Conference for World Peace at the Waldorf-Astoria Hotel in New York. It would become a benchmark in the early history of the Cold War. A kind of speed-dating relationship to American intellectuals, it was heir to the Popular Front of the 1930s and sequel to the World Congress of Intellectuals in Defense of Peace in Wrocław, Poland, the former German Breslau, the summer before. It attracted a superstar assemblage of some 560 sponsors. Science was represented, among others, by Albert Einstein and Linus Pauling, literature by Thomas Mann and Arthur Miller. From the pianist Artur Schnabel, the composer Aaron Copland and Leonard Bernstein to the jazzmaster Artie Shaw, the folk singer Pete Seeger and the *New York Times*'s Olin Downes, music in all its permutations was also well represented.

For many, its most memorable representative was a seriously uncomfortable Dmitri Shostakovich, who had been reprieved from near unpersonhood by Stalin himself to appear in New York with the Soviet delegation and read a speech that had clearly been prepared for him.[7] If only as faces in the chorus, Stern and his first wife, the ballerina Nora Kaye, were also sponsors.

Twenty years later, an inquiry arrived from Cedric Belfrage, a colorful figure in his own right as journalist, film critic, cofounder of a radical weekly and Soviet spy. Now relocated in Mexico after many years in the United States, he was working on a book about Joseph R. McCarthy, the Wisconsin senator who played anti-Communist Iago to a constituency of Cold War Othellos.

"I feel that 'a word from our sponsors' on developments in US intellectual opinion over this period would shed valuable light on developments in U.S. intellectual opinion over this period," Belfrage explained. He offered Stern a menu of options. "Do you now feel a) proud, b) satisfied, c) indifferent, d) ashamed of sponsoring the conference." In a minimalist reply, Stern opted for b).[8]

In the aftermath of the Civil War, the United States had considered buying Iceland. A year after the Waldorf conference, Stern and Zakin were again on their way there. During World War II, it was considered crucial to defense of the North Atlantic against German submarines. In the aftermath of the war in Europe, it remained a useful fueling station for bombers returning to the United States. Then came the Cold War. With Soviet bombers at least a theoretical threat, Iceland was again of interest to Washington as the eastern end of the so-called DEW (Distant Early Warning) line of radar stations and the site of a NATO base.

This time the tour was sponsored by Hurok. But the idea was the State Department's, which had recruited the American National Theater and Academy (ANTA), a New Deal creation, to initiate a cultural exchange program. There was no evidence of Soviet bombers on Stern's arrival. But a contingent of Soviet dancers and musicians, including the cellist Mstislav Rostropovich, had recently discovered Iceland too, and were not only performing, but touring from village to village, making friends and playing with local amateurs.

"We had just returned from a round-the-world trip," Stern recalled. "Getting back on a plane and spending Christmas week in Iceland was about the last thing in the world we wanted to do," he continued. "So we said yes."

As before, they played for a military audience that even honored the occasion by turning down the jukeboxes. But the real target audience was local, and so enthusiastic that it twice filled the 850 seats of Reykjavik's biggest movie theater; sold out the 650 seats of the local opera house, where Stern played the Mendelssohn concerto with the local orchestra; and crowded into a lecture hall at the university, where he volunteered an extra recital and question period for student listeners.[9] He then passed on his fees to the university to fund the acquisition of a music library.

As might be expected, his visit made an impression in Reykjavik. "Frankly, nothing has given me greater pride as an American citizen and as an official representative than having been a party to your visit here," the American head of mission informed him. His visit also made an impression in Washington, where the director of the State Department's Office of British Commonwealth and North European Affairs wondered if he might "come in and see us" when he was again in town.[10]

The idea took some getting used to. But it was increasingly clear to a cohort of postwar American artists that Iceland was just one of a world of countries waiting to be discovered by them. The new world self-evidently included Japan and India, where Stern and Zakin made their debut appearance in 1953, as well as Iran, where the State Department sponsored an appearance by Stern and Istomin in 1961.

En route from Manila to Calcutta, Stern reported his impressions of Japan. But it would become increasingly clear that his experience there was effectively generic. "In certain ways this could almost be called a diplomatic tour," he noted, "as we were always regarded as semi-official ambassadors of American culture."

At panel after roundtable after press conference, he and Zakin strove to show interest in the host country's people and traditions while emphasizing that Americans too could have dignity and cultural maturity. This was, he added, "something others are not always willing to grant us." As a parting gesture, they even set aside a share of the fee from their three last Tokyo concerts as a scholarship fund for young musicians.[11]

It was an irony of sorts that the geopolitical winds that blew Stern, Zakin and a platoon of Soviet artists to Iceland would also blow them to the Soviet Union their parents had left behind in 1921. Seen from the State Department, their triumph in Iceland was itself an argument for sending them ahead as America's pacesetters. They would appear in the Soviet Union four times between 1956 and 1966.

In March 1953, Joseph Stalin died after terrorizing the Soviet Union and much of the world for nearly 30 years. In July 1955, President Dwight D. Eisenhower of the United States, Prime Ministers Anthony Eden of Britain and Edgar Faure of France, flanked by their respective foreign ministers, convened in Geneva with Soviet Premier Nikolai Bulganin and Nikita Khrushchev, first secretary of the Soviet Communist Party. Their declared goal, so far as possible, was a thaw in the Cold War that had chilled most of the world since 1945.

Tangible achievement was elusive. But they at least brought back what would be known and recalled as the Spirit of Geneva. Before year's end, the great Soviet violinist David Oistrakh, a walking, talking personification of it, had not only been allowed to perform in the United States. In contrast to later Soviet artists, who were allowed to keep only 20 percent of their earnings, he was allowed to keep 50 percent of the $100,000 he reportedly earned.

Meanwhile, the *New York Times* reported from Moscow, the Soviet Ministry of Culture was negotiating, among others, for Stern. In Paris, *Le Figaro* unhesitatingly linked the report to the Spirit of Geneva.[12] "The Russians sent us their Jewish violinists from Odessa and we sent them our Jewish violinists from Odessa," Stern reportedly observed. He was widely quoted.

Neither official Washington nor official Moscow was amused. But the official invitation was well received by the State Department in January. Not usually known for his appreciation of soft power, even Secretary of State John Foster Dulles was impressed. Exchange of artists could only bring good to the world, he told a press conference.

At a closed session of the Soviet Party's Twentieth Congress in late February, Khrushchev delivered a denunciation of Stalinist tyranny that shook the Communist world. In late April, flanked as usual by Zakin, Stern arrived in Moscow, equipped with a del Gesù, a Guadagnini, cameras, heaps of film, and a reserve of Kleenex. His tour would include twenty-one concerts over twenty-seven days, eight of them with orchestra. In October, the Spirit of Geneva took a couple of hits when Hungary erupted in revolution against Soviet domination and Egypt's nationalization of the Suez Canal led Israel to join Britain and France in a quixotic war that threatened to become a Soviet-American confrontation. But by this time, Stern and Zakin were en route to Latin America.

"I believe with President Eisenhower that if the Russian people were to see the full picture of what is going on here, their suspicions that we are a belligerent country would be dispelled and there would be more respect and love between our peoples," Stern told Henry Raymont of the United Press on the eve of their departure for Moscow. He was also "expected to show Russia's music lovers that their cherished Oistrakh does not have a monopoly of virtuosity and musicianship," Raymont added.

The latter point was rhetorical, with no indication of whose expectations were meant. But their visit was hardly meant as a duel or a challenge. Far from competitive rivals, Stern and Oistrakh had been close friends and a mutual admiration society since 1951 when their paths crossed in Belgium, where Oistrakh had come to judge the Ysaÿe, later Queen Elisabeth, Competition and Stern to play in Antwerp. Accompanied by two "guardian angels," as Stern told an Italian interviewer,[13] Oistrakh had come to hear his concert and get acquainted. They agreed to meet again in Brussels, where Stern was reluctant to visit the Soviet embassy and Oistrakh was not allowed to meet at Stern's hotel. They settled on the neutrality of a convenient café and chatted for five hours.[14]

The previous year, two weeks in advance of Oistrakh's Carnegie Hall debut, 7,000 people had already lined up by 8 A.M. for concert tickets that went on sale at 10 A.M. His experience in Boston, Washington and Chicago mirrored his experience in New York. "Reliably informed that there wasn't a violinist within 500 miles" who was not in the audience for his Moscow debut, Stern needed eight adjectives—perceptive, eager, knowing, warm, responsive, attentive, insatiable and affectingly demonstrative—to characterize his local audiences. In neither case should this have come as a surprise.

Attended by multiple delegations of official hosts as well as Daniel Schorr, then local correspondent for the *New York Times*, and a representative from the American embassy, Stern's arrival in Moscow was already a civic occasion. Zakin replied to the welcome speeches in Russian as fluently good as Stern's was fluently bad. They were then whisked off to the embassy for an interview with Ambassador Charles E. Bohlen in a bugproof room, where Stern reassured one of America's pioneer Soviet watchers "that I knew enough not to be persuaded by what I would be shown and told officially by the Soviet authorities."[15] On arrival at their hotel, they found Oistrakh and his son Igor, who had been waiting for them with a bottle of champagne and a jar of caviar for three hours.

Stern's impressions, as contained in a ten-page letter to the Hurok office and copied almost verbatim to the columnist Leonard Lyons, combine the immediacy of a *Life* magazine photo with the enthusiasm of a kid at summer camp. There was the *dezhurnaya*, the floor concierge, at his Moscow hotel, who listened to him practice till 4 A.M., hustled him into a hot bath, brought him tea and reminded him he had a concert to play. There were the doctor and medical team in Kiev who marched briskly into his hotel room, ordered him to strip, examined him, prescribed medication for a bad cold and fever, assured him he'd live, and marched out again the same way they had marched in. "All on the house," he added. There was the ceremonial wine consumption in Yerevan at a party hosted by the Armenian composers association that left him unable "to tell which chin held the Guarnerius."

There was also the garden party at the British embassy that ended in a near-contretemps when Khrushchev challenged the McCarran-Walter Act, which required that foreign visitors be fingerprinted. Bulganin naturally concurred. The requirement had, in fact, been waived for Oistrakh and subsequent Soviet visitors by the simple device of declaring their visits official. But Stern's dutiful explanation that the law was the law not only unleashed a storm from Khrushchev, but another from Hurok, who looked forward to importing Russians dancers after years of effort. "We will put our fingers around a glass," Bulganin declared. "We will put our fingers in yours to shake hands," he added. "We will never put our fingers on an ink pad."[16]

"To say that I am embarrassed would be putting it mildly," Stern wrote Bohlen on his return to New York. "If there was any diplomatic fumbling involved, it was on the part of Mr. Khrushchev," Bohlen replied in every sense diplomatically. "As I had already wired Washington, you handled yourself admirably . . ." Though it is hard to imagine that either Stern or Bohlen favored fingerprints, McCarran-Walter is conspicuously absent from the cascade of interviews that followed Stern's return, nor is there any mention of Jews. Two years would pass before the law was modified and the exchange reactivated.

Jan Peerce, the great American-Jewish tenor, was about to leave for the Soviet Union as Stern returned to New York. Stern was quick to brief him. With all affection for his colleague Oistrakh and warm feelings for the motherly *dezhurnaya* in the hotel, he knew a Potemkin village when he saw one. Don't talk politics, he told Peerce. Don't advise people. Don't play games with money. Don't talk to strangers. Assume that the walls of your hotel room have ears.[17]

But what impressed him most and what he most preferred to talk about on his return were audiences that couldn't get enough, and waited hours at the stage door to applaud, shake hands, present flowers, and thank Stern and Zakin for coming. Thirty police were needed to clear their way after a day that included two concerts of three concertos each, and a list of 22,000 for places in a 4,000-seat hall. "We took it as an almost inarticulate cry of their desire, their need, to feel contact with the outside world, particularly America, and we personified the target," he recalled.

In 1960, Stern and Zakin returned for a second tour. Unlike

the first tour, this one not only took them to the usual metropolitan centers and Baltic capitals, but Tashkent and Samarkand in the Soviet Union's Central Asian antipodes, where they talked to camel drivers and rode out an abrupt change in the geopolitical weather. On May 1, a surface-to-air missile brought down an American surveillance plane in Soviet airspace. The collateral damage included a scheduled summit meeting in Paris and an Eisenhower visit to the Soviet Union. Stern and Zakin played on undeterred while a road-show company, on tour as they were, played *My Fair Lady* to adoring crowds in Moscow.

But mail was waiting when he got home. Dated May 17, it was an Open Letter to American Colleagues that the press department of the Soviet embassy in Washington hoped he might find interesting. Signatories included Shostakovich, the conductor Kirill Kondrashin and the great ballerina Maya Plisetskaya.[18] "Imagine sending an air spy, that herald of the dark forces of war, over our land on our great May Day holiday, on the eve of the Summit Conference," it complained.

A still slipperier slope lay ahead. It occurred to him in June 1967, Stern told an Italian interviewer with a wink of understatement ten years later, that the Russians took a different view of Israel from his own. With Israel facing a coalition of Arab forces, massively armed and supported by the Soviet Union, it seemed self-evident that he should get himself to Israel, and just as self-evident that he not play in the Soviet Union. While lined up in late summer 1968 to play a benefit for Vice President Hubert Humphrey's presidential campaign, he was as appalled by the Soviet invasion of Czechoslovakia as he had been a year earlier by the Six-Day War. He only hoped that Hurok would initiate a global boycott. "I simply couldn't bring myself to play in the Soviet Union—not as a demonstration against the Soviet Union but as a sign of solidarity with the Czechs," he later told Potok. "It was seldom the case that music entered politics, but often politics entered music."[19]

The coming of Soviet-American détente failed to bring Stern back to the Soviet Union. But the Jackson-Vanik Amendment to the Trade Act of 1974 brought a high tide of Soviet-Jewish emigration to Israel, America and the attention of Stern. Soviet officials could talk to him again "when they allow their people to travel back and forth like any free country does," Stern told an Arizona interviewer in 1988.[20] Weeks after a failed coup against Soviet President Mikhail S. Gorbachev in October 1991, Stern finally returned to what had suddenly and amazingly again become Russia.

The discovery of Israel some forty years before had meanwhile changed his life. "I was never unconscious of being a Jew," he told Potok. But he conceded that he had barely been aware of Zionism until 1948, when Israel secured its independence. As so often, one thing led to another. Much as his friendship with Schneider had led to the endlessly consequential connection with Casals, his friendship with Bernstein now led to an equally consequential connection with Israel.

He'd known Bernstein since 1945. He'd already played with Koussevitzky, the iconic conductor of the Boston Symphony and Bernstein's patron. Bernstein, in turn, had got Koussevitzky interested in the Palestine Symphony, the Central European refugee orchestra created in 1936 by the great Polish-Jewish violinist Bronislaw Huberman, who had played Brahms for Brahms as a fourteen-year-old. Stern wanted to see Israel for himself.

In 1949, he got his chance when what was now the Israel Philharmonic invited "a young Jewish fiddle player from America" to play ten concerts with them, two or three concertos at a time from the repertory of eight, Bach to Tchaikovsky, he brought with him. "I played the whole goddamned repertoire," he told Potok. "I remember, of course, I didn't get any money."

What he got instead, much as he had from Casals, was a social, political and civic education like none he'd known to date, an intensive course in nation-building, and a sense of identity and kinship he'd never experienced. He arrived with minimal political awareness, he recalled, most probably in a piston-powered DC-6, a by-product of World War II with a cruising speed of 315 mph and a range of about 4,500 miles. The introductory experience would last him a lifetime. "Only after seeing the rest of the country, does one come to the realization that Tel Aviv is Jewish, but the rest of the country is Israeli," he reported. "And what a difference that implies—on the one hand all the neuroticism, and opportunism, so well known for centuries, and on the other hand, a radiantly healthy, alive, land-loving, immensely proud, and on the whole, fairly cooperative group of people who envy no one and have immense hope and confidence in the future."[21]

For a country eager for music and eager to connect with the world, Stern was the man for both. He was received with great expectations. By 1951, when he met Golda Meir, currently serving as minister of labor, he had met and made friends with most of the new nation's Founding Parents and much of the Ashkenazic establishment that would govern the country till 1977. It was not quite like being present at the creation. But it was close enough.

Over the next fifteen years, he would return to play with the orchestra seven times and even slip in a bit of Prokofiev and Bartók. By 1989, he estimated, he had visited Israel over a hundred times. In 1993, El Al, the national airline, bought ads in the major papers, showing a full-page image of a violin case with an El Al baggage tag. A discreet and dignified message at the bottom identified the owner for anyone in doubt.

ISAAC STERN

*For thousands of people each week,*
*the choice to Israel is the airline of Israel*

But there can't have been a lot of readers who failed to connect the dots.

The self-assured informality of Israeli audiences in shorts and khaki shirts, score in hand, immediately enchanted him. Like a visiting foreign minister or a new ambassador, which in a way he was, he was taken to meet the prime minister, David Ben-Gurion, who understandably impressed him. But he was equally impressed by a cab driver, who reminded him to get on with it because he had a concert that evening, and by Paula, the Founding Father's wife, who asked his impressions of "the old man" as she saw him out.

He remembered a midnight swim in Lake Kinneret with Teddy Kollek, who would become a close friend as well as a formidable mayor of Jerusalem. He also remembered tea, peanuts and conversation with a man "running agents in Lebanon" that followed at 2 A.M. at the house of a friend. In Jaffa, the general assigned to show him around told him war stories and explained his efforts to keep a promising young poet out of harm's way. The night clerk at a hotel in Tel Aviv that smelled of "urine and carbolic acid" wanted to know why he programmed Beethoven's Sonata, Op. 24, instead of Op. 96. In Haifa his hosts put him up in a sanitarium to assure that he got an egg for breakfast.

Nearly half a century later, in an appeal to the Seagram billionaire and philanthropist Charles Bronfman for continued support of the master-class project he called Encounters, Stern acknowledged both wistfully and painfully how much had changed since that life-changing first visit. "It is so different from the country I saw radiantly beginning its hopeful life in 1949," he sighed.

But it was clear from his sessions with Potok that the fading of that radiance had been on his mind since at least 1967, when one of the world's most spectacular military victories left a legacy of conflicts and dilemmas still unresolved years after Stern himself has left the earthly scene. Moshe Dayan, a native-born child of the first kibbutz as well as a storied military leader, understood the Arabs, he said. Meir, a child of Kiev and Milwaukee, who only recognized black and white, did not.

In 1967–70, as Stern saw it, Israel lost a unique opportunity to make its Arab neighbors an offer they couldn't refuse by integrating them into its economy, banking system and medical services. "Why didn't it happen?" Potok asked. "Golda didn't want it," Stern replied. Instead, there was another war in 1973.

Four years later, a watershed election in 1977 produced a new establishment, likely to wear a tie to concerts in contrast to their socialist predecessors, unlikely to invite Stern for a midnight swim in Lake Kinneret, and very different from the one that he had always known.

Thirty years after his discovery of Israel, it was clear why his remarks at a postconcert reception at the Tel Aviv Museum of Art made an impression. "Masses of Jews the world over have been hoping since 1948 that the State they have dreamed of and longed for has come into being," he declared in a follow-up interview with Rafael Bashan of *Yediot Aharonot*. "In recent years, more than a few of them have begun to doubt whether Israel is still the fulfillment of their yearnings."

He feared that intellectual standards were slipping and Israel was falling behind in the global competition for hearts and minds. He regretted that "a number of central figures" had not been called upon to set Jesse Jackson straight when the African-American presidential candidate included Israel on a tour of the region that also included Amman, Beirut and Damascus. On a recent visit by U.S. President Jimmy Carter, he was appalled by a meltdown of parliamentary decorum that even embarrassed Prime Minister Menachem Begin.

Sh. Z. Avramov acknowledged in *Ha'aretz* that Stern had a point. "At their meetings with government envoys today, leaders of the Jewish communities are totally taken aback by the steep decline of their personal and cultural standards as compared with their predecessors in similar positions," Avramov noted. For diaspora Jews, who regarded the early prime ministers, Ben-

Gurion, Levi Eshkol and Meir as leaders of the Jewish people, their successors were just prime ministers.

"Jews like myself will keep on coming to Israel," Stern told the interviewer from *Yediot*. "But—from now on we shall come here with fewer expectations and hopes than in the past." There was nothing new in what he said. The novelty was that it was he who said it, had planned ahead to say it, and assured the interviewer that he would unhesitatingly say it again. Spontaneously expressed in dialogue with Potok, his views on the new prime minister, Benjamin Netanyahu, were not flattering.

But whether at home or abroad, in the Israel of Ben-Gurion, whom he revered, or Netanyahu, whom he didn't, Stern was and remained the uncle from America who came when needed to do what he thought needed doing. Concerts were repeatedly canceled at the last minute to allow for hastily improvised wartime visits to military hospitals, for a concert on the newly liberated Mount Scopus and sixteen concerts with the Israel Philharmonic in 1967, and for more hospitals and an airbase in 1973. Like the famous gas-mask concert in 1991, he understood them as civic acts with music as an extension of policy by other means.

But this was true of virtually everything he did in Israel and for it. From 1982 to 1984, he was a natural go-to for NATPAC, "a bipartisan, multi-candidate political action committee that will back candidates from both parties on the basis of the candidate's concern for and position on the growth of anti-Semitism in the U.S. and the related issue of U.S. foreign policy in the Middle East." What was needed were $5,000 contributors who would also chat up their peers. Stern, of course, said yes. Of the eight

Democrats NATPAC targeted for support, six ran for president; one made it to the nomination, and he lost the election. Of five Republicans, one was reelected vice president. But the underwhelming outcome could hardly be blamed on Stern.

In 1993, Stern, and still more, his second wife, Vera, were again obvious candidates to round up American support for what was to be their friend Teddy Kollek's last stand. Very Friendly Advisor he called himself in a cover letter to the actor Kirk Douglas and his wife. Violin in hand, he even appeared on the street in Jerusalem for a photo op with the mayor, and incidentally collected about $200.[22] Stern had no illusions that Kollek would coast to reelection in a city where only one voter in four had supported his Labor Party at the most recent national election.

New York came through in style, with $25,000 from Bronfman, $10,000 from Marty Peretz, soon to be publisher of the *New Republic*, $5,000 from Felix Rohatyn, the banker who would save New York from bankruptcy in 1975, and $2,500 from James Wolfensohn, who would successively serve as chairman of the Carnegie Hall board, director of Washington's Kennedy Center and president of the World Bank. Jerusalem did not come through. Ehud Olmert, another improbable partner for a midnight swim in Lake Kinneret, was elected mayor, and another of Stern's Israeli landmarks was gone from public life.

But the institutional links, unmoved by tectonic shifts in the political landscape, would be his legacy. The first big question, clear since his visit in 1949, was how to help an infant republic survive and succeed. The second was how to put his unique package of personal skills, connections and temperament to practical use.

His answer was characteristically self-assured. On the face of it, Israel lived close to the edge. With enemies to the north, south and east, no dependable allies, an improvised defense establishment, an infant economy and no obvious natural resources, it was poor by virtually every measure of geopolitical power. But it enjoyed one crucial comparative advantage. Its neighbors might have oil. Israel had talent.

Stern's first priority was to persuade a small country, in existential need of support and legitimation from anyplace likely to regard it as "us," that its musical talent was as much a strategic asset as its aptitude for enterprise, organization and science. His second was to persuade its movers and shakers that he was the man to locate, develop and leverage that talent.

In a remarkable medley of manifesto, position paper and shopping list, dated Tel Aviv, October 1961, he then took on the question of how. The text of some 3,000 words on nine closely typed pages is specifically identified as a draft, and no addressee is indicated. But the opening paragraphs alone made it clear that he was aiming high and thinking big.

"This outline is based on acceptance of the following facts," the paper began. Communist utilitarianism had turned the arts into a public utility and a vehicle for propaganda. "The emergence of Red China, . . . a threat as yet unrealized by most of the West," meant a reassertion of its own ancient traditions. Add an ascendant postcolonial Africa, and "Western Civilization as we know it . . . [was] on its way to extinction unless drastic and immediate action is taken by those concerned with the traditions that bore us and bred us."

This was where Israel came in. "Externally, the trained talent and the setting of standards in civilized life can become, after immediate attention to necessary defense needs, Israel's most powerful export and its most meaningful image to the world at large."

"Internally," he continued, "it can mean the assurance of Israel's existence, according to the dreams and hopes of Jews everywhere, as an ethical, cultured and intelligent force." But an obligatory "or else" came with the rhetorical territory. "Only through the awareness of the Government and its willingness to act now can the possibility of Israel sliding into a Levantine civilization be averted."

What followed was a national project, centralized and coordinated in a ministry of culture, buffered by advisory committees and open to suggestions, which were not long in coming. Prominent among them were a national academy with an elite faculty for aspiring pros; a scholarship program, including foreign study, for the best and brightest; a cadre of foreign orchestra players to raise even the standards of the Israel Philharmonic né the Palestine Symphony; a training orchestra in Haifa; a first-rate chamber orchestra at the Israel Broadcasting Authority; a purchasing authority to buy ten Steinways; incentives, of course, for patrons and philanthropists, and a budget approximating 10 percent of total educational spending.

"It can mean no less than the saving of Israel," he concluded. To his delight, the brigadier general and particularly innovative helicopter pilot who happened to be the Israel Defense Forces' director of education, saw it that way too. "He thinks of the

Army as the most important single school in the country," Stern told a British friend, "and feels profoundly the absolute necessity of a wide cultural base for this educational power."[23]

Violinists Pierre Baillot in Paris and Joseph Joachim in Berlin had something similar in mind when they created conservatories with the same heft and sense of national mission as Saint-Cyr, France's West Point, and the Preussische Kriegsakademie. But so far as is known, neither the French nor the Prussian Army maintained a string quartet, an Excelling Musicians program that allowed draftees to continue their studies while on active duty, nor a commanding officer like Vadim Gluzman's, who ordered the twenty-five-year-old Gluzman, the oldest soldier in his unit, to two hours of daily violin practice in an air-conditioned van as after-hours "punishment."[24]

Echoes of Stern's preamble were still audible in Philadelphia some fifteen years later, where he had come to address the local chapter of the America-Israel Cultural Foundation. Created in 1939 to support the Zionist project in Palestine, it now brought Israel's best and brightest to the conservatories of Philadelphia, Boston and New York.

A few months earlier, Israeli commandos had rescued 102 of 106 hostages, whose flight from Tel Aviv to Paris had been diverted to Uganda by Palestinian and German terrorists. The operation was a notable victory in the global battle for hearts and minds. But even goodwill had a limited shelf life, Stern cautioned, and the IOUs were again rolling in. "The arts offer megatons of power too often neglected," he reminded his listeners.

Save for the obligatory reference to the arts, the message could as easily have been a pitch for the United Jewish Appeal or the Litchfield County Hadassah. But for Israel and Israelis, a radical makeover had successively turned the grand design of 1961 into a prospectus, a work in progress, and a functioning institution.

The idea behind the makeover surfaced in early 1971 in an interview with the broadcaster Martin Bookspan, commissioned by the American Jewish Committee as part of an oral history project. But it had clearly been gestating over an extended period. "How do you see yourself and your future intertwined with what may happen in Israel in the next quarter-century?" Bookspan asked. What he had in mind, Stern explained, was a "loose institute" where "some of the leading artists of our time" would teach the teachers.

Talent was no problem, he continued. "The problem now is to be able to train their young people, within their own country, so they don't have to leave the country . . . and the greatest talents do not stay away from there and then divorce themselves from the State's development."[25]

A few months later, the "loose institute" reappeared as a structured proposal. There was to be a teaching faculty of five, including a "world famous pianist, a virtuoso cellist," as well as two violinists, one conductor, plus Stern himself. It would start with four student pianists, violinists and cellists, as well as two or three violists, recruited by competitive audition. Ad hoc chamber groups were to be combined and recombined so that all students interacted with all faculty. A "good secretary," ideally with a car, as well as a coordinator and a studio pianist for the string players, were also needed. There were to be three "large, bright" studios, ideally soundproofed, with a concert-quality Steinway in each of them. There was to be housing and practice space for the student players as well as twenty-five to thirty teacher-auditors. If it worked for two years, "it would then be clear what will be needed to create a more permanent establishment."[26]

Remarkably, it did and was, thanks to a gang of three and a casebook-worthy demonstration of synergy in action. First among equals, Stern wanted demand for what he also wanted to supply. Kollek, visionary mayor of an imperfectly reunited city with millennia of contentious past, wanted a future. Isaiah Berlin, the Oxford political philosopher, whose passion for music cohabited with a passion for Israel, Jerusalem and a robust sense of Jewish history, welcomed an opportunity to help both Stern and Kollek.

Their respective CVs enhanced their credibility and added value to their IPO. Stern, the uncle from America, knew the art, the business and the world like few in the history of the profession. Like few of his peers, the pragmatist Kollek understood what was needed to turn one of the most contested urban spaces on earth into a modern city whose adversary communities might at least agree to coexist. Berlin, a close friend of both Stern and Kollek, was also a friend and advisor to Dorothy Mathilde de Rothschild, whose family foundation was a pillar of Kollek's Jerusalem Foundation.

Created in 1965, the foundation was a one-of-a-kind philanthropy funded by foreign donors to establish green spaces and secular cultural institutions in a city in serious need of both.

After almost twenty years of neglect and partition, the Mishkenot Sha'ananim, established by the philanthropist Moses Montefiore in 1860 as the first neighborhood outside the city walls, looked like a priority candidate for rehabilitation. With its emblematic windmill, it also looked like an optimal home for Stern's field of dreams.

In 1973, the Jerusalem Music Centre opened for business. Place, time and occasion are preserved in a fifty-seven-minute film by Ruth Leon and Paul Salinger. Half historical document, half video scrapbook, it would be screened eighteen times total on fourteen public TV stations from Boston to Seattle within four weeks of its release. Nearly half a century later and two and a half years after its appearance on YouTube, it would be viewed almost 11,500 times more.[27]

In its opening sequence, the camera hovers briefly over the city, the Israel Museum, and the Dome of the Rock. It then leads up the steps to the windmill and the unassuming entrance of the new building.

As expected, if Stern built it, they would come. And so they did. Stern, of course, appears front and center with Schneider close behind. There are cameo appearances by Stern's trio partners, Rose and Istomin, as well as Artur Rubinstein. The pianists Gina Bachauer and Claude Frank are seen like Stern himself in individual and small group tutorials. Energized as though he were fifty years younger, even Casals appears just months before his death at ninety-six to conduct a student orchestra, play a bit of solo Bach for Golda Meir, and challenge Ben-Gurion, a mere eighty-seven, to an affable chat about longevity. Meir saw the film on Israeli TV in one of her last conscious hours, Stern was told later, and it was one of her happiest experiences.[28] As part of the institutional family, Kollek and Mrs. de Rothschild make cameo appearances too.

But the film's most important players, both musically and cinematically, are the students, outstandingly gifted pianists and string players from preteen to draft age, totally engaged in an experience that combines the rigors of a lesson at Juilliard or Curtis with a summer at Marlboro. A testimonial to the admission process, the teenagers selected for attention by Leon and Salinger in 1973 were still active at the top of their profession a half-century later. The pianist Yefim Bronfman, seen here at seventeen, would go on to a brilliant solo career while performing and recording with Stern as a successor to Zakin. Bachauer, beaming, is seated next to Bronfman at the piano. Stern is heard chuckling avuncularly.

He had every reason to be pleased. But it came as no surprise to anyone who knew him that Stern was a man who made things happen. His career in public citizenship was in fact already in its second decade. Like charity, it had also begun at home. In spring 1960, Robert E. Simon Jr., who had inherited Carnegie Hall from his father in 1935, announced its impending demolition. For everyone concerned, it was the moment of truth for which Stern would be best remembered.

"The struggle to save Carnegie Hall was a watershed in my life," Stern would tell Potok almost forty years later. "It taught me things about myself I hadn't known before: I could sway influential people through speech; I had the ability to stir crowds not only with music but also with words: I possessed an instinctive ability to navigate with some skill the tricky waters of politics and power."[29]

Conceived in 1887, the hall was a happy conjunction of civic demand and private supply. The demand side was represented by Walter Damrosch, then twenty-five, and heir to the New York Symphony and New York Oratorio societies founded by his father. The supply side was represented by Andrew Carnegie, fifty-two, the hugely rich industrialist-philanthropist who would go on to fill the American landscape with public libraries and endow the World Court in The Hague. The city needed a world-class concert hall, Damrosch explained. Carnegie got the message, and the Music Hall that was renamed for him only a few years later opened spectacularly in 1891 to an audience whose carriages lined up for a quarter-mile outside. Over the next sixty-nine years, it would serve as a platform for artists of every kind from Paderewski and Kreisler to Benny Goodman and Duke Ellington, as well as public figures that included Margaret Sanger, Mark Twain and Winston Churchill. But the sky darkened perceptibly in the mid-1950s.

First, Robert Moses, known, not always admiringly, as New York's "master builder," proposed renewal of Lincoln Square, a "plebeian" West Side tract a few blocks from Carnegie Hall, as a complex of cultural institutions to be called Lincoln Center. A consortium of the city's movers and shakers, among them John D. Rockefeller III, fell in behind him.

A second challenge to the hall's future came from inside the building. In 1925, Carnegie's widow had sold the hall to Robert E. Simon Sr., a New York real estate investor who summered at his Long Island country home or ranch in Arizona when he didn't take his family to Europe. On his death in 1935, the building passed to his son. A self-described "Jewish guy from Manhattan," Robert E. Simon Jr. was also a recent Harvard graduate, an amateur pianist and a music lover. Long since iconic, Carnegie Hall had even been a moneymaker. But the music world had changed over twenty years and the bottom line had moved, too. For decades, the New York Philharmonic had been Simon's principal tenant. It now announced plans to move to Lincoln Center.

The cost of maintenance was already cause for concern. More remunerative use of a well-situated location in midtown Manhattan was another. Simon's dream of the new model suburb that would become Reston, Virginia, and the land acquisition needed to make it come true, was a third. By the mid 1950s, Simon felt himself forced to sell Carnegie Hall, ideally to a buyer as concerned to save the building as he was. Yet even at the relatively modest asking price of $4 million, the equivalent of about $38 million in 2018, public appeals and ad hoc search committees got nowhere. Approached by Stern about the possibility of a joint venture with Lincoln Center, John D. Rockefeller III said no.

In 1956, Louis Glickman, a prominent developer, took out an option on the site. In September 1957, an architects' sketch of the proposed replacement, a forty-four-story office tower, clad in red porcelain, appeared in *Life* magazine. Stern referred to it as "the red terror." Then even the option was dropped, leaving no alternative on the table but demolition. It was already early January. The wreckers were expected by the end of May.

At this point, Stern went into action. "It slowly became clear to me that what was really necessary was some kind of road map that would enable us to resolve the issue politically," he would recall in his memoir.[30] It was an insight of potentially secular consequence. But if it were to work, it called for an effective activist with the resources and connections to turn Stern, a committee of one, into a critical mass. A decade earlier, Schneider led Stern to Casals. This time, he led Stern to Jacob M. Kaplan, also known as Jack, a man of many philanthropies, extending from the arts and human rights to neighborhood redevelopment and public transportation.[31]

An entrepreneurial alchemist, Kaplan had left school at sixteen to turn a succession of enterprises including the Oldtyme Molasses and Welch Grape Juice companies into gold. He then turned the gold into a remarkable portfolio of civic causes, among them the New School, where Schneider was director of an in-house concert series. Stern explained why the city had to be persuaded that Carnegie Hall was not a building, but a civic, even a global, icon. Kaplan was receptive to the argument. He would think about it, he said.

In January, Kaplan and a few close associates who would become the Citizens' Committee for Carnegie Hall, assembled in Stern's nineteenth-floor apartment. Well heeled and widely experienced, they were a colorful lot. Frederick W. Richmond, a subsequent recruit, had made his way through college as organizer and pianist of the Freddie Richmond Swing Band en route to a fortune in business. Colonel Harold Riegelman had served in both World Wars, been adopted by a Philippine family as an honorary uncle, and reluctantly accepted appointment as acting postmaster of New York at the request of President Eisenhower.

It was no coincidence that they also personified another New York institution, a balanced ticket. Richmond, as deputy finance chairman of the Democratic National Committee, knew his way around Democrat-dominated City Hall. Riegelman, who had run as a Republican candidate for mayor of New York, knew his way around the Republican-dominated State Capitol in Albany. Eleanor Roosevelt, with her son John, was another welcome recruit, as was Hurok. So was Albert S. Bard, whose pioneer Bard Act of 1956 provided legal protection for the first time to "places, buildings, structures, works of art and other objects having a special character, or special historical or aesthetic interest or value."

There was no question that Carnegie Hall qualified, the editorial board of the *New York Times* announced on March 21. The next day, between entries on Cuban-American misunderstanding and *The Visit*, Friedrich Dürrenmatt's "not very pleasant" theme and variations on vengeance, misanthropy and urban renewal, Mrs. Roosevelt concurred in her syndicated column.

In a reader's letter a week later, a third civic lion, Richard S. Childs, vice president of a nonpartisan Good Government lobby, also weighed in. But he was strenuously opposed. Not only were two full-size halls more than the musical traffic would bear, he insisted, but "Thanks to modern science," the new hall's acoustics could be just as good as Carnegie's.[32] Experience would show him wrong twice over. Lincoln Center's Avery Fisher Hall required multiple makeovers in its first fifteen years. No one before or after said "practice, practice, practice" when asked how to get to Lincoln Center.

In any case, Childs was already outgunned. While Riegelman and State Senator MacNeil Mitchell, Carnegie Hall's man in Albany, took on the legislature, Stern opened a second front with a telegram to Mayor Robert F. Wagner Jr. in City Hall. "I am hopeful that I will have early opportunity to explain to you in person why it is so important that New York City act to preserve the great institution of Carnegie Hall."

A few days later there was another salvo, cosigned by twenty living legends, among them Fritz Kreisler, age eighty-five, Pablo Casals, age eighty-four, Artur Rubinstein, age seventy-three, and Van Cliburn, the twenty-six-year-old superstar, whose victory in 1958 at the premiere Tchaikovsky Competition in Moscow had earned him a ticker-tape parade on his return to New York. "In the minds of civilized men everywhere, it is the gateway to musical America," the letter declared.[33] "To destroy it now for 'practical reasons' is an act of irresponsibility damaging to the United States and our prestige in the entire civilized world."

In its April 9 issue, *The New Yorker* hailed Stern, "not hitherto known as a military genius" as a local hero for his efforts to date.[34] A few days later, Stern and Mayor Wagner met at an ecumenical seder. Invited in for an ecumenical beer on their way home, the mayor confirmed warm feelings for Carnegie Hall extending back to his childhood. He was even an honorary member of the musicians union. But it was clear to both that what happened in New York was contingent on what happened in Albany.

A week or so later, in the last days of its annual session, the legislature passed two bills essential to the survival of Carnegie Hall. Both John D. Rockefeller III and his brother Nelson were founding trustees of Lincoln Center. As governor of New York, Nelson had even steered $15 million of the state's World's Fair budget to Lincoln Center as designated host to the Fair's performing arts program. But unlike his brother, he also came to the rescue of Carnegie Hall by signing the bills crucial to its survival.

The first, prepared by Riegelman as counsel for Stern's Citizens' Committee, allowed the City of New York to buy, improve and modernize Carnegie Hall, and lease it to a nonprofit corporation that would finance the necessary makeover with bonds. The second, introduced by Mitchell, extended similar protection to all such sites. On learning of Rockefeller's decision, the venerable Leopold Stokowsky interrupted himself while conducting a children's concert. "The large audience of parents and children cheered for three minutes," the *New York Times* reported. "Carnegie Hall is saved!" Stern informed Rubinstein, and presumably all other colleagues who had leaned on the mayor in the common cause, in an appreciative note dated June 9.[35]

On June 30, in the presence of Mayor Wagner, Richmond as chairman of the corporation and the singer Marian Anderson as representative of the art, the city took title to the building for a purchase price of $5 million to be amortized over thirty years and leased it to the corporation. In 1964, in the presence of Wagner, U.S. Secretary of the Interior Stewart Udall, and Stern, the building was designated a national landmark.[36]

Within months of Carnegie Hall's rescue, America elected John F. Kennedy, the first president to make a poem and its poet,

Robert Frost, part of his inauguration. Before the year was over, he had personally appealed to Casals to modify his boycott of countries that recognized the Franco government in Spain.

"I look forward to an America which will reward achievement in the arts as it will reward achievement in business or statecraft," Kennedy declared in a speech at Amherst College just weeks before his assassination. No president had said anything quite like that before nor has any said anything quite like it since. "And I look forward to an America which commands respect throughout the world not only for its strength but for its civilization as well," he continued. He could have been channeling Stern. As the producers of *Music at the White House*, a film shown on public television forty years later, would recall nostalgically, these were "years when artists were welcomed through the front door as honored members of the Republic."

It was "a time of possibilities," Stern would remember on camera a quarter-century after the assassination. "With him you could always believe in the ninth inning home run, winning the fifth set at Wimbledon, making a three-and-a-half minute mile, in having all the children in the country be able to read, write and paint and dance, be able to speak many languages . . ."[37] Along with the Voting Rights Act—and Vietnam—public funding for the arts was among the possibilities he left to his successor, Lyndon Johnson.

It was not quite necessary to start from nothing, nor the first time the federal government had made an effort, common in Europe, to underwrite the arts. A variety of projects—music lessons, ethnomusicology research and thirty-four orchestras included—had supported unemployed artists between the mid-thirties and the early years of World War II. One of the orchestras, the Chicago-based Illinois Symphony, even drew a crowd.[38] But for most, save the artists themselves, art was a means to an end, and public support ended with the war and full employment.

The challenge was persuading a fully employed, resoundingly prosperous and increasingly college-educated postwar America to do the same. "Perhaps no country has ever had so many people so eager to share a delight in the arts," Kennedy reported in a piece published under his name in *Look* magazine in late 1962, complete with glossy paper photos of an intensely earnest Rudolf Serkin rehearsing with an unseen conductor, and an equally earnest Stern practicing in his bathrobe.[39]

Ancestors of what would become the Kennedy Center were spotted before the end of the Eisenhower Administration. The first year of the Kennedy Administration brought another novelty. In August 1961, concurrent with the Berlin Wall crisis, the arts intersected with public policy, the rubber met the road, and a dispute over orchestra wages threatened a crisis at Lincoln Center. Secretary of Labor Arthur J. Goldberg, a future Supreme Court justice, had represented striking Chicago newspaper workers, the United Steelworkers and the Congress of Industrial Organizations in its merger with the American Federation of Labor. He was now called on to mediate between the Metropolitan Opera and the American Federation of Musicians. His intervention saved the coming season. He incidentally proposed that government subsidize the performing arts.

In 1962, Kennedy appointed August Heckscher, formerly

chief editorial writer for the *New York Herald Tribune* and later the city's Commissioner for Parks, Recreation and Cultural Affairs, as a first-ever special consultant on the arts. A year later, with a presidential advisory council in view and Stern among its members,[40] Heckscher returned to his post at the Twentieth Century Fund. But he left a report, "The Arts and the National Government," that attracted bipartisan support from the kind of senators other senators listened to.

Thanks first to Mrs. Kennedy and the president's press secretary, Pierre Salinger, then to Supreme Court Justice Abe Fortas, a good amateur violinist, close advisor of Johnson, and a personal friend, Stern was at least indirectly present at the gestation. He was even invited to meet Johnson himself. "Isaac," Johnson reportedly told him, "I don't know from beans about the arts, but you and Abe tell me this is a very important thing to do, and so I think it's important, and I will back it, and I promise you I will keep my cotton-pickin' hands off it."[41]

In the summer of 1964, Congress endorsed and Johnson signed legislation for a cultural center in Kennedy's name, as well as a National Council on the Arts with subcommittees for each of them. On September 29, 1965, Johnson signed the National Foundation on the Arts and the Humanities Act, thereby establishing the National Endowment for the Arts. To no one's surprise, Stern was among the first round of presidential appointees when the council convened in 1965.

A few months later, the Endowment, with a budget of $2.5 million and a staff of fewer than twelve, issued its first grants. The first eighteen grants to music and musicians, comprising about 40 percent of the total, went to composers, the New York Opera for development of young talent, orchestras in Denver and Boston, and ethnomusicology projects. Two years later, the winners included Schneider, concerned as always with the deficit of young string players, and a couple of programs aimed at violin repair and analysis of historic varnishes.

The Council experience brought Stern another network of connections, including the choreographer Agnes de Mille and the actor Gregory Peck, who would remain his friends for the rest of his life. As maître de plaisir at Stern's seventieth birthday celebration in San Francisco, Peck happily recalled a Stern proposal for a $4,000 grant to enable a New York maker to pass on the formula for his unique artisanal rosin to an apprentice. The proposal led to a four-hour debate. "You can imagine who won," Peck added, again to no one's surprise.

But win a few, lose a few, there was also the learning experience of observing what could happen when a small pie was served at a large table occupied by people as smart and competitive as himself. Stern and Warner Lawson, music dean at Howard University, shared an interest in a music teaching method for elementary school pupils invented by the Hungarian composer Zoltán Kodály. Stern had seen it work in Israel. Both wanted to adapt it to the American scene. They proposed a $50,000 grant to send ten experienced music educators to Hungary for training. They would then come back and act as multipliers. The proposal was accepted. Investment in the project eventually reached $91,000.

Stern's other proposal for what he called a master chamber orchestra was both ingenious and fatally flawed. Senior players from the major orchestras were to show up for two years, alternate in leadership positions, then go home, ideally as seasoned leaders and better for the experience. As a group, they would meanwhile concertize and tour places that rarely saw an orchestra.

Schneider was already advertising for candidates with salaries and benefits few orchestras could match. Not surprisingly, the orchestras protested what they saw as seduction of their best and brightest with public money, plus unfair competition from a government-sponsored ensemble. Not only were they already talking to their congressmen, their trade association, the American Symphony Orchestra League, also demanded that their leadership write directly to the president himself, and claim a place on the Council.

Orchestra trustees were often campaign contributors. But they were not negotiating from strength with a president who had carried forty-four of fifty states in living memory en route to reelection. It seemed likelier that such a letter would only make Johnson the more adamant in defense of the Council he had personally nominated and whose independence he had guaranteed. Anyway, dissenters were assured, opposition from the established orchestras would itself suffice to kill Stern's project. Despite strenuous opposition from Stern, this turned out to be true.

The episode is unmentioned in his memoir, as is another setback some years later when unexpected outrage caused a scheduled outreach to exceed Stern's grasp. Since 1980, the New York Philharmonic had played an annual concert at Harlem's Abyssinian Baptist Church, an institution dating back to 1808. Midori and Shlomo Mintz, both Stern protégés, had even appeared there as soloists.

In December 1986, with Stern as scheduled soloist, 41 of the orchestra's 106 players struck. The year before, the famously anti-Semitic Louis Farrakhan, leader of the Nation of Islam, had appeared at Madison Square Garden. The players were upset that Abyssinian Baptist's executive minister had failed to protest.

As a matter of personal principle, Stern refused to play in Germany, but he played in Harlem. As a matter of principle, the orchestra players who refused to play in Harlem, while on tour in Europe had played in Germany.[42] Reaction was mixed. "No entire group is responsible for the beliefs and actions of a few," said one correspondent. "I want you to know that I will not attend any more performances at Carnegie Hall, nor shall I purchase any of your wonderful recordings," said a second. "I think that Jews, no matter how liberal, have responsibility toward fellow Jews," said a third.

But setbacks, be they in Harlem or in Congress, rarely set Stern back for long. "In time to come, we may also realize the necessity of providing assistance to the arts not necessarily on the federal level but on the local level," he'd presciently told an Oklahoma audience in 1964.[43] That was true too. Johnson's Great Society had long since gone the way of Kennedy's New Frontier. Legislators not only made the National Endowment a favorite piñata; they made sure that there was little in the piñata they wanted to smash. But music education and public funding remained among Stern's priorities.

An indignant letter to New York Governor Mario Cuomo

in 1989 protesting an $8.5 million cut in the state arts budget was characteristically eloquent, if a little shaky on the physics. "America has become the focal point of the distillation of the best of Western culture," he wrote. "And New York, State and City, is the center of that strength."[44] In 1995, a Minnesota state senator thanked Stern for his impact on fellow legislators on a recent visit to St. Paul[45] and the "significant difference" it made on the annual arts council appropriation

In 1999, an Isaac Stern School of Music surfaced—and vanished—among a set of ten career-specific charter schools, including an automation center and a school of animation arts, proposed by Rudy Crew, chancellor of the New York City Board of Education.[46] A year later, Stern, like his friend Frank Sinatra, did it his way.

In May 2000, age seventy-nine, Stern invited the city's forty-three school superintendents to Carnegie Hall for a half-hour violin lesson after their monthly meeting with the chancellor. The idea originated with Harold O. Levy, Crew's interim successor, who was intent on encouraging more music instruction in the city's 1,100 schools. Many were apprehensive on arrival, but most were eager for more by the time they left.

"This is the opportunity of a lifetime," said Matthew Bromme, superintendent of District 27 in Queens. "I was very excited to be in his presence," said Paula LeComte Speed of District 18 in Brooklyn. He was thrilled to contribute, said Stern.[47]

IV

# Chairman of the Board

"WHOEVER WANTS TO KNOW THE HEART AND MIND of America had better learn baseball," the historian Jacques Barzun noted in a much-cited essay in 1954.[1] Whoever wants to know the heart and mind of America over eight decades of Henry Luce's American Century,[2] could do worse than reflect on the careers of Isaac Stern and Frank Sinatra. At first glance, they might seem the definitive Odd Couple. On closer inspection, they could as easily be considered among the century's avatars.

Born poor to immigrant parents, both would live to be awarded the Presidential Medal of Freedom, Sinatra in 1985, Stern in 1992. "New York, New York," and "My Way" could have been composed for either of them.

Save for a few years' difference—1920–2001 in Stern's case, 1915–98 in Sinatra's—they were almost immediate contemporaries. Sinatra was a school dropout. Stern had hardly dropped in. Both discovered their musicality and calling at an early age. Both were classified 4-F, ineligible for military service in World War II, in Sinatra's case because of a perforated eardrum. But both toured military bases at home and overseas with USO troupes.

From the end of the 78 rpm era to the threshold of digital recording, both were tireless and prolific recording artists. For some years, they even shared a company. Both showed an unanticipated aptitude for Hollywood. Like Stern, Sinatra included Israel in his support for liberal causes.[3] At least until 1972, when the singer switched registration, both were generous supporters of Democratic presidential candidates. Both were serially married, Stern three times, Sinatra four.

From the eve of World War II to the eve of the twenty-first century, their careers proceeded in parallel. Both, in fact, had regularly appeared at Carnegie Hall since the 1940s, when Stern played his breakthrough recital and Sinatra appeared at a campaign rally to endorse President Roosevelt.

That 1960 was a significant year for both was another noteworthy parallel. It was also a year in which their trajectories diverged. After six years with Columbia, and nine with Capitol, Sinatra founded Reprise, a record company of his own, where friends like Dean Martin and Sammy Davis Jr. enjoyed the same unrestricted creative freedom and ownership that he did.[4] Three years later, reportedly heavy weather caused him to sell two-thirds of the company to Warner Brothers, though he retained a seat on the board.[5]

Stern remained happy with Columbia and its successors until the end of his career. He meanwhile tended to the salvation of the iconic property at the corner of 57th Street and Seventh Avenue, New York, New York, where he would remain king of the hill, top of the letterhead, until his death in 2001. In 1965 he added the presidency of the America-Israel Cultural Foundation, which continued to list him and his second wife Vera, another managerial force of nature, as chairmen in memoriam after their passing.

Ironically, it was Sinatra who was popularly referred to as chairman of the board, although he wasn't one. Stern was occasionally referred to half jocularly, half enviously, as godfather to a family of protégés known popularly as Kosher Nostra, despite names like Midori Goto, Cho-Liang Lin, Sarah Chang, Jaime Laredo and Joseph Swensen not usually associated with matzoh ball soup and pastrami sandwiches. But no one was known to call Stern president, although he really was one.

Clear to everyone, irrespective of what he was called, was what and how much he did as one of the world's master networkers, one of the world's master multitaskers and designated go-to guy for an astonishing number of causes and purposes.

That he and Sinatra converged again at Carnegie Hall seemed counterintuitive. But it should not have come as a surprise. Where, if not Carnegie Hall, did people who could draw a crowd go to do it? Where, if not Carnegie Hall, would Sinatra take his storied Rat Pack buddies, Dean Martin, Joey Bishop and Sammy Davis Jr. on January 27, 1961, to raise money for the Southern Christian Leadership Conference?

A generation later, Sinatra was back, this time to raise over $250,000 for the house itself. The evening of June 4, 1984, was memorable in part for an audience that included Donald J. Trump and his then-wife Ivana. It was also memorable for a plumbing malfunction in the Second Tier restrooms that flooded the most expensive boxes.[6] Two years later, now seventy-one, Sinatra returned for still another benefit.

By this time, a master plan for restoration and renovation had been in the works since 1979. In 1982, with a mandate from the board, an ad hoc committee submitted a rather different master plan for renovation and revision of the building's mission statement.

If the idea looked familiar, it was probably no coincidence. Twenty years earlier, Stern had proposed a national chamber orchestra that Schneider had even started to recruit.

In 1968, Carnegie Hall became available and Schneider performed CPR on a project once considered DOA. His New York String Orchestra Seminar, still going strong fifty years later with cosponsorship by New York's New School, had meanwhile become a holiday institution. There were even modest grants from the National Endowment for the Arts.[7] In 1982, the proposed Carnegie Hall Academy for Advanced Musical Performance was also reconfigured as a kind of MBA program for aspiring orchestra players with an all-star faculty and a collateral program of adult education.[8]

"Since the program would be under the aegis of Carnegie Hall and is widely known to be a consequence of Isaac Stern's personal interest, his deep and personal interest in the shaping of the program is viewed as indispensable," the report emphasized. It was obviously a crucial paragraph.

But for the moment and the foreseeable future, air-conditioning ducts and restrooms had priority. In 1986, the board, whose chairman, James Wolfensohn, was as redoubtable as Stern himself, agreed that the time had come for a makeover on a scale not seen since Carnegie Hall opened in 1891. The goal, as Stern defined it, was "nineteenth-century elegance with 21st-century plumbing."[9]

As early as 1966, Eugene Ormandy, the veteran conductor of the Philadelphia Orchestra, had complained about onstage temperatures of a 100 degrees Fahrenheit on a day when the outside temperature was 88.[10] "The ceiling was starting to come down, the air conditioning and the elevators had to be replaced and there was much cleaning and repainting to be done, as well as changing old seats, and in general, trying to give a fresh look to the hall in its 95th year," Stern explained to Potok.[11]

It was challenging enough that it had to be done between mid-May and mid-December, the longest break Carnegie Hall could afford without renting space and selling tickets. A second complication was the need for specialists with the rarefied skills needed to restore the Gilded Age plaster on the ceiling and iron grillwork over the whole building. A third complication was a repair schedule that allowed only two months to organize the gala reopening intended as the light at the end of the tunnel.

The good news was Stern. In principle, he had already been there and done that a decade earlier, when the Hall celebrated its eighty-fifth anniversary. In four months he'd performed what without him might have been the work of two years, persuading five superstars—Leonard Bernstein, Vladimir Horowitz, Mstislav Rostropovich, Stern's San Francisco contemporary Yehudi Menuhin and the baritone Dietrich Fischer-Dieskau—to arrange and rearrange their schedules in order to perform at what was modestly called "the Concert of the Century."

Hand in hand with Wanda, Horowitz's wife and Toscanini's

daughter, he teared up as Fischer-Dieskau sang, accompanied by Horowitz, while Bernstein turned pages and Rostropovich leaned against the piano. A famous photo shows all of them, including Stern and Julius Bloom, the hall's executive director, happily belting out the Hallelujah Chorus from Handel's *Messiah*.

For the makeover celebration in 1986, he turned again, as he did so often, to Bernstein and Zubin Mehta, conductor of the New York Philharmonic, for help with the civic version of a society wedding, a union of the art of politics with the politics of art. At 6 P.M. on December 15, Mayor Ed Koch, accompanied by a contingent of the city's social establishment, arrived in a horse-drawn carriage to cut the ribbon. As father of the bride, Stern hosted ex officio. Like a Cold War summit or a victory in the Super Bowl, the story appeared on the front page of the next morning's *New York Times* with art on three columns and a sidebar on the obligatory party that followed the concert.[12]

With tickets at $50 to $2,500 a seat, the musical main event extended at least three hours. Long since an institution himself, Sinatra was a natural candidate for the program. The New York Philharmonic, a Carnegie Hall resident until it decamped for Lincoln Center in 1962, shared the first third of the concert with Horowitz, another institution who had made his Carnegie debut when Stern was eight; Bernstein, who made his Carnegie debut, like Stern, in 1943; as well as Yo-Yo Ma, the mezzo-soprano Marilyn Horne, and Stern himself.

Horowitz played Chopin. Bernstein conducted Bernstein. Ma performed a movement of Haydn. Stern joined Horne in the aria "Erbarme dich" from Bach's *St. Matthew Passion* with its transcendent violin obligato and a text that translates as "Have mercy." For anyone inclined to brood, the message was at least ambiguous, particularly coming from the president of the corporation and the evening's closest approximation of a maître de plaisir. But it was not an evening for brooding. Wagner's Overture to *Die Meistersinger* led emphatically from Bach to the first intermission.

The next third of the concert was given over to Sinatra. Known for his association with people of interest to the Department of Justice, the evening's second meistersinger also chose repertory that touched the subliminal. "Mack the Knife" began life as a Weimar-era hymn to a Georgian era highway robber. Was it too dog whistle a message for the 2,812 concertgoers who filled the hall to capacity? "New York, New York," with its celebration of "a city that doesn't sleep," was easy by comparison. Much of the audience then went home to bed.

For those who remained as midnight approached, the orchestra, the New York Choral Artists, Horne and the soprano Benita Valente all returned for the evening's finale, the last movement of Mahler's Second, *Resurrection*, Symphony. Once again there was text—"Rise again, rise again you will, my dust" by the German poet Friedrich Klopstock—with an arguable subtext. After a half-year of secular renovation, the text's reference to rising dust did not require much postmodern deconstruction either.

For those who stayed and paid, there was still more to come. Fifty to five hundred dollars bought a ticket to the concert and a view of the newly spiffed-up interior. A thousand dollars bought a champagne reception in the lobby. For $1,500 more, there was a buffet. Most exclusive of all was what the *New York Times* described as "a small post-performance supper" of caviar, smoked salmon, medallions of veal, French pastries and champagne by Veuve Cliquot in the company of Ma, Bernstein, Mehta, Wolfensohn and Stern with their respective wives and Sinatra.

Not everyone was happy about the last of the featured performers. "There has been and [will] probably continue to be a spotlight for the pet and handiwork of the American Mafiosi, but how in the name of sanity he fits in to the new frame that you have provided is beyond belief or rationale," wrote one disgruntled customer. "Someone at Carnegie Hall ought to be discharged for this." Similarly, "the news that Frank Sinatra will be one of the honored guests and performers at the rededication of Carnegie Hall tarnishes the event and cheapens it," wrote a retired Columbia University sociologist.

If the first two messengers conveyed genteel outrage, a third reported unintended farce. Spectators watching the audience arrive from the other side of 57th Street looked up at what appeared to be the Dress Circle ladies' room, where they spotted "a very attractive lady . . . with her skirt raised to her waist." Unsurprisingly, both the ladies and gentlemen on the sidewalk below burst into giggles. "The windows were opaque . . . but unfortunately, not opaque enough," Stern's informant added helpfully.

Presidentially quick to show where the buck stopped, Stern replied almost immediately and at length in defense of Sinatra. "It was the most natural thing in the world to choose him," he explained coldly. The program was meant to showcase classics in their respective fields, Sinatra among them. "Over the years, he has been a staunch friend and admirer of Carnegie Hall . . . ," Stern declared emphatically, who "has performed there regularly, and has given of his time and money to the rebuilding efforts." There were also plenty of people in the classical field "you might not always want as guests at the table," he added. With a copy to Stern, a senior staff member reassured the correspondent that the windows were also being attended to.

By now, respectful collegiality had morphed into outright cordiality. As a guest at Sinatra's Palm Springs home, Stern noted with interest that his host could whip up a spaghetti sauce for fifteen with the same skill and dedication that he himself brought to his favorite borscht for six.[13] He also recalled with gratitude how Sinatra presented him a "double packet of tubed Cuban cigars" in 1986, the year of the great makeover.[14] Since 1962, Cuban cigars had been under embargo, even when bought in third countries. How Sinatra's gift got through U.S. customs remains a nice question.

The 1986 overhaul itself was a metric of how Stern's presidency had evolved since 1960. Yet another confirmation that virtually anything at Carnegie Hall was news fit to print, Leslie Bennetts recalled a kind of teaching moment years earlier.[15] A would-be donor had offered Carnegie Hall a huge organ. Someone else had accepted in Stern's absence. "Over my dead body," Stern declared on his return. Carnegie's legendary acoustics were and remained a supreme and perennial preoccupation. No one on his watch, Stern explained in 1983, was going to risk them by busting into the walls to install an organ. It was a unilateral decision he and only he could make. In the beginning, Wolfensohn recalled, Stern, his wife Vera, and Julius Bloom, the managing director, ran the place like something of a mom-and-pop shop. A generation later, no one any longer made unilateral decisions.

Programming policy alone was a radical change. Since it was built, Carnegie Hall, like the Concertgebouw in Amsterdam, had been a kind of parking garage that rented space to performers and their managers. It now did its own programming, which increased from under 10 percent of the year's total in 1970 to over 27 percent by 1982–83.

Over the same period, staff increased from 10 to 46, with professional managers in charge of public affairs, marketing, real estate renovation and development, accounting, fund-raising and strategic planning. Board members, once Friends of Isaac, were now sought out by a nominating committee and put up for election. Record-keeping had advanced from 3x5-inch cards to computers, donors from 541 to 7,196. Managing director, once a solo position, had been split in two, with an artistic director as the other bookend.

In a ferociously competitive market and profession, where conflicts of interest were not unknown, it was widely believed by some, some notable violinists among them, that Stern had favored his protégés over others, predominantly American-born or naturalized, who were equally gifted and had also practiced, practiced, practiced. The pianist Earl Wild, who had often played at Carnegie at his own expense, but never been engaged by Carnegie Hall, devoted a full chapter of his memoirs to Stern's presumed animus against American artists in general, and himself in particular.[16]

The staff of, course, denied it, as did Stern, and Wolfensohn insisted that Stern only saw the coming year's program in the spring when the board did. They could hardly be expected to say anything else. But there was no conclusive evidence either, no memo, e-mail, wink or smoking gun, to prove this untrue.

Though grateful to be out of day-to-day management, Stern continued to exhibit an active concern for acoustics, board membership, fund-raising, and goodwill in both the public and the private sector. The 1986 makeover was cause enough for concern about the acoustics. The sixty-story Carnegie Hall Tower, intended as a follow-up to the makeover with luxury condos, office space and assured rental income, was cause to attend to the goodwill of City Hall.

In 1987, Carnegie Hall's director of development, Lawrence Goldman, prepared a list of talking points for Stern's appearance before the Board of Estimate, a kind of municipal steering committee that included the mayor. The "poetry," he said, was for Stern to work out. But his instructions on what Stern should and shouldn't say were clear and emphatic.

Certain areas were best avoided, Goldman warned. There should be no discussion, for instance, of how many dollars the project would bring in. It was very (underlined) important to thank the board "for their past and constant support." Stern should point with pride to how far the city and Carnegie Hall had come together in twenty-eight years. He should tell the board, as he told everyone else, that the new building "will be standing for 100 years and must be something we can be proud of."[17]

At the same time, independent signals from messengers as

different as *The New Yorker*'s Andrew Porter, the pianist Alfred Brendel and Robert A. Kadison, CPA, a multiple subscriber,[18] called his attention, like it or not, to a very different challenge. As all three reported credibly and at length, the Hall's legendary acoustics had sustained collateral damage from the great makeover that would take more than talking points to correct.

"The management of Carnegie Hall is not unmindful of some of the reactions of listeners to the sound quality after the completion of some of the renovations which restored the Hall and gave it the necessary strength to last another hundred years," Stern replied a bit defensively. But help was on the way, he reassured the writer, in the form of "very specially designed acoustical screens which we will be putting up in a variety of formations in the coming months . . ."[19]

Years later, Carnegie held a news conference to announce the new screens. Allan Kozinn, then a music critic for the *New York Times*, recalled that, when questioned about reports of concrete under the stage, Stern peevishly insisted that the sound in the hall was just fine—it was only journalists complaining, he said, and blamed any deficiencies in what critics heard on their seats of choice, where they could better be seen. They sat in the seats Carnegie assigned to them, the critics replied. Stern then issued a challenge: "We'll take up the stage to look for the concrete," he said, "if your newspapers pay to replace the stage when we don't find any."

None of the journalists were empowered to commit their employers to such an arrangement, but several years later, the critics were reconvened for another press conference, at which

Judith Arron, the executive director, reported that there was indeed concrete under the stage floor, and that it was discovered only because the workmen had failed to install a vapor barrier between the concrete and the wood. The stage was therefore leeching water from the concrete, and had to be replaced.

The acoustical screens announced by Stern at the earlier press conference not only cost $10,000 in 1988 dollars; there was also a consensus that they had not helped a great deal. When it turned out that the stage had to be replaced because of the concrete/vapor barrier problem, Kozinn asked Arron if any legal action was planned. The answer was no. He then noticed that a substantial number of major contributors and board members were either in building or real estate.[20] The 1986 building makeover shows up in Stern's memoir. The acoustic makeover it required does not.

While the acoustic problem was eventually met and solved, money remained a perennial challenge for an aspiring institution with expansive plans, a growing staff, and no endowment. The investment in professional staff paid off in expertise and strategic thinking that might have impressed the Joint Chiefs of Staff. Trustees, carefully screened, paid off in networks as well as personal donations. Donors led to more donors. The buck, and lots of bucks, stopped and frequently started with Stern, who kept track, so far as possible, of "annual giving, major commitments, ticket purchases and general work for the Hall."[21]

It was probably an oversight that no one proposed "Donate, donate, donate" as an alternative answer to the emblematic question "How do I get to the Carnegie Hall board." In any case, it would only have been a beginning.

A checklist for prospective trustees identified three categories of eligibility. The first, "Senior executives of major corporations," were expected to show a particular interest in arts philanthropy, demonstrate a proven record of corporate giving, pitch in at least $100,000 annually of their own or other people's money to the Annual Fund, and raise an additional $250,000 to $1,000,000 in special cases like Endowment Fund drives.

The second category, unaffiliated private "Individuals," were expected to pony up $5,000 to $10,000, make themselves useful on committees, buy benefit tickets and raise $100,000 to $500,000 for the Endowment Fund when asked.

A third category, "Artists and Educators" were off the hook for money but expected "to lend their stature to specific Carnegie Hall programs, and use their ability to articulate the Hall's mission to help cultivate and solicit donors."

Assuming they'd gotten this far, candidates were then interviewed by at least two members of the nominating committee. It was hoped that they knew a few board members already. They were then put up for a vote.

Prospective donors were also categorized. The Endowment Fund enjoyed priority. Top prospects were understandably assigned to Stern. All of them were board members. A representative set in 1993 included Brooke Astor, a pillar of the civic establishment and serial philanthropist, as well as Annette de la Renta, the wife of the designer, who was also a candidate for the endowment campaign steering committee. A second set of trustees, presumably waiting on deck, included the entertainer

William H. Cosby Jr., popularly known as Bill, and Richard Debs, a hugely networked international investment banker, who connected Stern with Edward Said, the Palestinian activist and literary critic, another unlikely pair of dots.

Briefing books were a wonder to behold. All visits were preceded by dossiers that addressed virtually everything of interest and potential relevance short of blood type—personal history, family connections, education, business history including net worth, public office and civic activity, trusteeships, philanthropies, art collections, honors and foreign decorations.

Donor potential in the range of one to five million dollars was, of course, prominently noted. But so were strategies the staff considered likeliest to succeed. "The key point to convey to **Mrs. Astor** [in boldface] is that you hope Carnegie Hall will be the recipient share of the remaining $23 million in Astor Foundation assets," Stern's briefer, Susan Shine, suggested.

She thought it possible that Mrs. Astor might also help with Ms. [Annette] de la Renta, and reminded Stern that he had already offered "to speak candidly to Annette about providing Carnegie Hall access to members of her social circle." Beside asking her to help with others, Stern could "assess when to ask for her own (and Oscar's) financial commitment," Shine added. "We will of course be delighted to help in any way we can to arrange meetings, concert evenings and other opportunities for you to be with these prospects," she assured him.[22]

In 1963, the eighteen-year-old Itzhak Perlman made his Carnegie Hall debut. A year later he won the Leventritt Competition, the concert world's version of the World Series. Stern's discovery and where it led was a leading indicator of how one Stern presidency led to another.

Since the coming of Heinrich Wilhelm Ernst and Joseph Joachim in the mid-nineteenth century, Ashkenazic whiz kids from Eastern and Central Europe had been to the violin what Italian tenors had been to the opera. A few, like Yfrah Neaman and Ivry Gitlis, had even come from Mandatory Palestine. But Perlman was the first unequivocal Israeli. Just 12 when Stern discovered him in 1957, he became an instant sensation a year later when an estimated 11 million viewers tuned in to Ed Sullivan's wildly popular TV variety show to watch him perform with a mixed platoon of young Israeli pianists, singers and dancers. At forty, he had good reason to express handwritten thanks to Stern and his wife Vera for "being with me most of my life" and "being my friends."[23]

But practically from the beginning, it was clear to Stern that there was more and comparable talent where that came from. It was just as clear that the talent was a developable resource in search of a developer. He estimated that some 3.5 million Israelis needed a year to generate the cultural activity that New York and London generated in a week. Development was not only in the public interest. It was in the national interest.

Like the mandate to save Carnegie Hall, the mandate to create and invent the Jerusalem Music Centre was essentially self-conferred. As he was in New York, Stern was a necessary, but not a sufficient condition. Again as in New York, his project presupposed a collaborative mix of public sector, private sector and philanthropy, in this case mostly foreign.

With nothing to compare it to, explaining his vision could be a challenge. But explaining what it was for was comparatively simple, even in a city where simple was a little less common than snow.

Was it a conservatory, a master class, music's version of a Florida try-out camp? Was it a Silicon Valley startup, vertically integrated with the America-Israel Cultural Foundation, that connected Israel's best and brightest with the great American conservatories and the promised land of a professional career? The answer was, well, not exactly. But traces of all of them could be found in its genome, and its uniqueness could even be a comparative advantage. It was also registered as a charitable trust.

"The newly formed Jerusalem Music Centre is an attempt in Israel to overcome the isolation that distresses most of this nation's classical musicians," Lois Applebaum Leibow reported in 1976. "Quietly opened, this center is designed as a meeting place where Israeli musicians can learn from the world-renowned performers who visit." She acknowledged the state-of-the-art recording studio as essential to the videotape library that figured large in Stern's Grand Design. She also pointed to "the help of a $2.5 million grant from Yad Hanadiv (Memorial to the Benefactor), the Israeli arm of the Rothschild Foundation, that was essential to Stern's role as initiator and prime mover.[24]

"Isaac is probably the hottest property in the musical world today," Frederick Gash, a fan and New York philanthropist, declared in 1977 in a proxy appeal to the president of the Alcoa Foundation, urging him to support the project too. Still in his mid-fifties, Stern "could work 1001 nights a year at $10,000 per engagement," Gash added in case his point was missed or challenged.[25] Yet in addition to everything else, Stern expected to spend six to eight weeks a year at the Centre, Leibow reported, and he hoped to persuade colleagues as heavily booked as himself to make themselves available for labor-intensive visits of two to four weeks each.

In time, like its colleagues in New York, an increasingly professional staff took over most of the heavy managerial lifting. But there was no question who was and remained the go-to guy of last resort, even on such micromanagerial issues as negotiating donation of sound equipment with Mickey Schulhof, the vice chairman of Sony, and acquisition of a concert-quality Steinway.[26] The minutes of a 1981 board meeting, forwarded to Stern in London, extend over ten single-spaced pages of stenographic typescript. Among issues discussed, many of them left open, were current activities and future plans; the care and feeding of visitors such as pianists Lili Kraus and Alfred Brendel, soprano Christa Ludwig and violinist Sergiu Luca; how the board should relate to a CEO, currently referred to as manager; what it should expect in the future of a CEO, to be known as director; a recent orchestra workshop as well as a recent workshop for composers; a broadcast policy and recording project, and the next year's budget. But the pivotal sentence, added with pencil, was the last one. "Next meeting should take place in May when Isaac is in Israel."

For all the obvious differences between New York and Jerusalem, the presidential skills appropriate to one were also appropriate to the other. It was also in the nature of the relationship that names that showed up at Carnegie Hall should show up at the Jerusalem Music Centre too.

Jerusalem or New York, Stern needed people, be it as board members with cash and connections, as managers to deal with the contingencies of day-to-day and season-to-season operation from plumbing to payroll, or as artists to deliver the goods at the highest level to students and subscribers. Manhattan or Mishkenot, there were also the inescapable imperatives of cash flow. Common concern for propagating the gospel of great music, as well as a common concern for finding a saleable product led in turn to a shared interest in technology and media markets.

The Jerusalem board was already a little work of art. Seven members—two from Yad Hanadiv, one each from Kollek's Jerusalem Foundation, the Jerusalem Symphony and the America-Israel Cultural Foundation, plus Kollek himself and Jacob Rothschild as chairman—clearly represented local constituencies. Then came the public representatives, among them Lilian Hochhauser, the veteran British impresaria, and Lady Jill Ritblat, a passionate supporter of the arts, who was conveniently married to Sir John Ritblat, chairman and CEO of the British Land Company.

Had it stopped here, the board would already have been recognizable as a New York–style balanced ticket. But three more members sufficed to qualify it for nomination to a Networkers Hall of Fame. One was Sir Isaiah Berlin, the most celebrated intellectual of his generation. The second was Sir Claus Moser, director of Britain's Central Statistical Office, chairman of the Royal Opera House and warden of Wadham College, Oxford. The third was James Wolfensohn, who would go on to be chairman of the Carnegie Hall board, chairman of Washington's Kennedy Center and president of the World Bank.

Unlike Stern's representatives in New York, the universally popular Arron and the universally unpopular Franz Xaver Ohnesorg who was her successor, Ram Evron, a veteran broadcaster and director of the Jerusalem Music Centre, seems to have been the candidate of consensual pragmatism. Some of the board found him deficiently imaginative. But no one, and certainly not Stern, seems to have questioned his competence. "It seems to me that the Music Centre is at present functioning exceptionally well," Stern told the board in 1985. "Largely as a result of the present Director's devoted and particularly able management . . . ," he added.[27]

In 1991, Evron resigned briefly to pursue an outside offer, and ninety candidates reportedly appeared to take his place. He then asked the board to rehire him, which it did. One of Israel's major papers, *Yediot Aharonot*, considered the attendant drama fit for two columns. *Ha'aretz*, Israel's answer to the *New York Times*, considered it fit for three.

The center that Stern had proposed as fervently as Theodor Herzl had proposed a Jewish state had meanwhile become its own little Zionist metaphor. "If you want it, it's not a fairy tale," Herzl had once proclaimed. "If we build it, they'll come," Stern might have added. All kinds of programs for all kinds of participants now went on, in effect, around the clock and around the year with a steady stream of world-class visitors as coaches and role models.

"I was so touched by the warmth of your reaction at the end of our conversation when I felt the beginning of a dream perhaps becoming visible," Stern wrote Serkin as he invited him for two months in Jerusalem over the turn of the year 1972–73. "Four students at the most and absolutely top quality already able to play at finished levels."

But whose nickel? This was where the money came in. "We cannot be in a position to ask professionals to subsidize their activities in Israel, nor can we presuppose Pro-Israeli sentiments as a basic factor in the minds of gifted professionals around the world," he reminded Arthur Fried of the Rothschild Foundation.

What happened next was Las Vegas in reverse. What happened at the Music Centre was not meant to stay at the Music Centre. On the contrary, it was supposed to preserve the art, even improve the world. Outreach, for example, adaptation of Hungary's folksong-based Kodály method to Israel, was at the heart of Stern's grand design. This was also true of archival preservation that would make the visits of Casals, Serkin et al. as accessible to future generations as a library book. But both projects only increased the need for state-of-the-art capital investment and professionals who knew what to do with it. Even thoughts on marketing the workshops and coaching sessions in viewer-friendly, made-for-TV format meant spending money to make money.

"The Jerusalem Music Centre is not an easy place to work, either in terms of equipment or personnel," Stern's film producer, Ruth Leon, warned a New York colleague. "One has to have a great commitment to Israel, a personal obligation to the Centre, and a limitless sense of humor to withstand its vagaries,"[28] she noted. But it was worth the wear and tear. "Isaac was such a quick study, he could grasp anything that interested him immediately, including the more obscure aspects of our rudimentary television technicalities," she recalled decades later.[29]

As Janet Aviad, the director of Bronfman Philanthropies reminded him, the Centre could not be entirely depended on to sell itself. Charles Bronfman, the Canadian-American philanthropist, for example, was not "overtly enthusiastic, as far as his money is concerned, for 'elitist' projects . . ." Aviad thought it might "prove a brilliant idea if you were to persuade him of the long-term benefits for Israel ensuing from this venture." Evron suggested that Stern talk to him personally in Jerusalem. As so often, Stern's magic seems to have worked. "Bronfman's foundation has committed itself to the program," Fried notified Evron. "Only a jack-ass would not understand the obvious."

Never one to pass up an opportunity, Stern was even known to hit up total strangers like the president and CEO of the Liberty Vegetable Oil Company in mid-flight. Kollek then continued where Stern had stopped. "Isaac Stern wrote me of his propitious plane trip where he had the good fortune to meet you and discuss with you the possibility of helping us with the distribution of the 30th anniversary concert videotape . . . ," he wrote.[30] By now, the Centre had become a part of the landscape, and the next loan or check could wait a day or week without existential risk.

An unaudited overview in November 1992 estimated that two-thirds of the Centre's funding came from Rothschild, and 15 percent from the America-Israel Cultural Foundation. An overview on the eve of 1993 estimated revenue at $996,787, expenditures at $925,441. "Annual income twenty pounds, annual expenditure nineteen and six, result happiness." Dickens's Mr. Micawber could have been speaking of dozens and hundreds of artistic and philanthropic enterprises But he could also have been speaking of the Jerusalem Music Centre.

As real and present in Israel as they were not in most other places were the respective challenges of a citizen army and an exodus of some 350,000 mostly Jewish immigrants from the Soviet Union between 1989 and 1992. Of these, 11,000 claimed to be artists, and 60 percent of them said they were musicians. Specialized skills were unevenly represented in Israel as they are in most small countries and many large ones. But whatever Israel's deficits, orchestra players were not among them. A fifty-two-year-old immigrant cellist was reported to be playing seven hours a day on the street.[31]

Neither the draftee musician nor the underemployed orchestra player was unique to Israel. Armed with a French horn, Charles Dancla, later professor of violin at the Paris Conservatory, had dutifully reported for militia service after the revolution of 1848. Between 1952 and 1962, aspiring American musicians could meet their service obligations in the Seventh Army Symphony, a full-sized ensemble deployed in Stuttgart. But save for the very Orthodox, Israel made no exceptions. Service, in principle, was universal. Musicians served with everyone else, with no provision for their practice schedule.

Like Alexander Glazunov, director of the St. Petersburg Conservatory, who spent days negotiating residence permits for little Jewish prodigies with Czarist bureaucrats, Stern was regularly summoned to negotiate accommodations with the Israeli military authorities. Like Glazunov, he was generally successful. He was also delighted with Brigadier General Nechemiah Dagan, the army's new director of education and "the most attractive and dedicated person I have met in this post during the last 20 years."

Fried confirmed his enthusiasm. "The possibilities for us to work productively with the army are almost limitless," he reported to Stern. He proposed regular visits to the Centre by soldiers on days off in Jerusalem and the loan of library tapes to bases around the country.[32] He brain-stormed happily about concert series at Army bases and looked forward to a chat and coffee with Dagan's staff officers already scheduled on the eve of the next board meeting.[33]

The Russians were regarded rather as a civic obligation than as an opportunity. Western clichés to the contrary, they were not all Perlmans and Philadelphia Orchestra players just waiting to be discovered. Stern dealt with them pragmatically, case by case. Together with Schneider, he toured startup chamber orchestras, including the Israel Camerata in Rehovot that would be among the immigrant successes. Meanwhile, Fried approached David Rockefeller about money to support them. There were workshops at the Music Centre for Russian teachers. Like Perlman and Zukerman before them, a few of the newcomers like Bronfman and Gluzman qualified for membership in Stern's professional family practically on arrival. A born candidate for Stern's version of tough love, Gluzman was informed that everything he did was wrong. Like the commanding officer who ordered him to practice, Stern then assigned him to play two years as second violinist in a string quartet, where he learned to listen to the other players. Gluzman remained eternally grateful.[34]

By now, people who had once wondered why the Jerusalem Music Centre was needed and what it was good for wondered how they had got along without it. The cellist Amid Peled recalled how the Centre had led to the America-Israel Cultural Foundation, which had led in turn to years of study at the New England Conservatory with Bernard Greenhouse of the Beaux Arts Trio, a professorship at Baltimore's Peabody Conservatory and a career. "Without Stern, I'd still be farming on my kibbutz," Peled said.[35] Stern was his best teacher, Peled recalled. He not only wanted young players to do things. He asked, and made them ask themselves, why they did them.

Ivan Stefanovic, a longtime member of the Baltimore Symphony, recalled a master class at the Cleveland Institute years earlier, where Stern asked a student to tell him why she played a passage in the Tchaikovsky concerto in a way that had not occurred to Tchaikovsky. The answer was "Tradition."

"Let me tell you about tradition," Stern replied. He then told about the man who relieved himself for lack of alternatives in the middle of a field. Others, who saw what he had done, did the same. The results were predictable and cumulative—in four letters. "That's tradition," Stern said. Stefanovic passed on the story to his own students exactly as he heard it. "And they never forget it," he added.[36]

After Israel came East Asia, both retail and wholesale. Like his relationship with Europe and Israel, Stern's relationship with Japan extended over almost half a century. He was already hailed as something of a culture hero on arrival for his first visit in 1953. In 1971, the *Asahi Shimbun* with its 10 million daily readers included him among the 100 "most influential figures of today's America" selected to answer a questionnaire on the state of U.S.-Japanese relations, prepaid return postage included.

Asked to choose three or four items from a menu of twenty-two qualities he considered most characteristic of Japan, Stern bent the rules and opted for nine. Among them were energetic, polite, tough bargainers, highly competitive, education-minded, nationalistic, like to do things together in groups, physically strong and skilled craftsmen.

Asked his views on Japan's remarkable recovery and economic success after the devastation of World War II, he acknowledged that American aid was a necessary condition, but not a sufficient one. "The principal reason," he continued, "is the industry and training and desire for high standards evidenced by the Japanese themselves, their vision in seeing they had to enter and match the technology of the twentieth century as quickly as possible in order to survive and maintain a major position in the world economy." Experienced Stern-watchers often remarked that he would also have excelled had he gone into business or politics instead of music. Diplomacy was a possibility too.

In 1997, he returned with the Baltimore Symphony to deliver "a passionate performance of Bruch's G minor Concerto to a wildly appreciative audience," visit music schools, hear young musicians and "dispense sage advice." By now, he was practically a national institution.[37]

In 1983, Japan also came to him in the person of Midori Goto, age eleven. She had already auditioned for Mehta and performed with the New York Philharmonic. "Miss Dori [*sic*] was one of those young people who has obviously been trained to play like a little grown-up," Bernard Holland noted reflectively in the *New York Times*.[38] "It was more than a little sad to listen as this lovely, brilliant young girl tried so hard to act as if she were one of us." It was not Stern's custom to address fan letters to music journalists, he declared. But in this case he made an exception. "Your feelings about the young Japanese girl, Mi Dori [*sic*] were so perceptive, so intelligently right and so to the point that I could not but send these few words and say a quiet bravo!" A few weeks later, she was standing in his apartment, accompanied by her teacher, Dorothy DeLay. She was "one of the most extraordinary talents I'd heard in the past 40 years," Stern recalled in his memoir. "I determined to take a personal interest in her development,"[39] he told himself, and did, beginning with a letter to Akio Morita, the chairman of the Sony Corp.[40]

"I think she is one of the rare talents that will proudly present Japan's musical achievements in our day world-wide," Stern told him. Lee Lamont of ICM Artists, who would later be Stern's manager, passed on a similar message to Sony's CEO Norio Ohga, who would acquire Stern's home company, CBS Records, formerly Columbia Masterworks, a few years later. A first season in Aspen led to an invitation to play a Vivaldi concerto for three violins with Stern and Zukerman in St. Paul. Honorary granddaughter to the one and kid sister to the other, she was not even a teen-ager. In time, Stern would also lead her to his physical therapist, conveniently located in Carnegie Hall,[41] and to dealers, collectors and patrons who would help her borrow, find and pay for a great instrument.

Their recollections of one another are curiously asymmetric. Though few, references to her in Stern's memoir are unfailingly positive. References to him in her memoir advance from As-Seen-by-an Adolescent-Through-a-Glass-Darkly, to mature respect and appreciation for concern and patience unmatched by anyone else while she worked her way through an extended personal crisis.[42]

Like Midori, Stern's first China connection also came to him, but this time it was in Paris. Since the memorable days in Prades, Étienne Vatelot, the Paris luthier whose shop was Paris's answer to Hill's in London and Wurlitzer in New York, had been a close friend. As DeLay alerted Stern to Midori, Vatelot alerted Stern to Yo-Yo Ma, age seven and scarcely larger than his cello. On tour in Europe in 1962, Stern agreed to hear him. Once again, an audition became a eureka experience.

Soon after the Ma family emigrated to New York, where Ma's father taught at the École Française, which the Stern children also attended, Stern sent Yo-Yo, already nine, to study with Rose. As Vatelot had introduced Ma to him, Stern now introduced the boy to Hurok. Then, as Monteux had done for the sixteen-year-old Stern, he recommended Ma to five major-league conductors. All said yes.[43] As was usual in such cases, "without our asking, without our even knowing it," he had "simply gone ahead and done it," Ma recalled in what amounted to an 1,800-word birthday card that appeared in the *New York Times* on the occasion of Stern's seventieth birthday.[44]

When Ma was seventeen, Stern invited him to play the great Schubert cello quintet with the grown-ups—himself, Schneider, Zukerman and Rose. It was a heady experience. But it was years before Ma thought to ask why "a great artist would want to play with someone 35 years younger."

The question was not only a challenge to Ma and the circle of protégés who also enjoyed Stern's most-favored status. It was a challenge, even an affront, to others who considered themselves equally qualified and failed to make the cut. There were at least four answers to account for it. None necessarily excluded the others.

The first and simplest was that Stern and presumably his colleagues already considered Ma a mature player. The second answer, which was Ma's, was that generosity was Stern's nature, "but the other person has to meet him halfway," which Ma evidently did. Since someone, somewhere, almost always raised the question of whether and how Stern figured in other people's lives, a third answer showed up in an interview with Shlomo Mintz, another of his Israeli protégés. Did Stern have the power to block careers and prevent people from playing in the United States? "I think helping people interests him more than the opposite," Mintz replied, and he already had his hands full with Carnegie. He was doubtful that Stern had the time to stand in someone's way.[45]

A clue to the fourth answer could be found in Stern's role some years earlier in the Leventritt Competition, at the time America's most exclusive. By unwritten convention, the judges awarded one prize or none. Yet in 1967, contrary to all precedent, Stern persuaded his colleagues to award two first prizes, to the Korean Kyung Wha Chung and Pinchas Zukerman. His intervention reportedly raised eyebrows, even hackles. Yet it would have looked familiar to any academic doctoral supervisor, who did everything possible to support an unusually gifted student.[46]

Like Vatelot's tip on Ma, the year 1971 also led to China, when Henry Kissinger, then President Richard Nixon's national security advisor, visited there. As top secret as top secret can get, the visit was America's first official contact since 1949, when Mao Tse-tung's Communists evicted Chiang Kai-shek's Nationalists, America's longtime client. In 1972, Nixon himself visited China. This time the visit was public as public can get and an international sensation. In 1973, the Philadelphia Orchestra visited China, another icebreaker. In 1979, Isaac Stern visited China.

The idea was his own. An approach to Kissinger, who by this time was no longer in office, was a nonstarter. Then luck struck again. Learning that a chemist neighbor had invited the Chinese U.N. Ambassador and later Foreign Minister Huang Hua to dinner, Stern got himself invited too.[47] Huang had been professionally interested in the United States since 1958. Like millions of Americans after a thirty-year blackout, Stern was keen to see China. One invitation led to another.

In June 1979, he arrived for a three-week tour. The ten-year Cultural Revolution, China's version of revolutionary France's *Terreur*, had ended only three years earlier. Among Stern's gang of some twenty were his family and his pianist David Golub, as well as a film crew recruited for the occasion by Walter Scheuer.

Chairman of a New York investment company, Carnegie Hall trustee, longtime patron of the arts and a Friend of Isaac, Scheuer was effectively starting from zero, with no previous experience of either the art or business of moviemaking. Save for one scene, nothing was rehearsed, and everything was shot in real time, Stern told Potok. Money, at least, seems not to have been a problem.

They brought back sixty hours of film with neither a script nor a storyline. After a fallout with Scheuer, there was no director either. With no way to go but up, Scheuer hired Murray Lerner and Allan Miller, both respected documentary filmmakers, to turn his lemon into lemonade.

Legend had it that the dancer Isadora Duncan proposed to the dramatist George Bernard Shaw that, with his brain and her body, they should produce a baby. But what if the baby inherited her brains and his body, Shaw reportedly asked?

"I like to think that 'From Mao to Mozart' proves, at the very least, that with Isaac Stern's body and my brains one can make a very nice little film," Scheuer wrote an acquaintance.[48] Meanwhile, he himself mastered the business with such success that he would go on to produce seven more films,[49] including *Small Wonders*, a little masterpiece on Roberta Guaspari, a charismatic Harlem Suzuki teacher, that ends with a Carnegie Hall recital and even a cameo appearance by Stern.

It took a year for Lerner and Miller to reduce sixty hours to eighty-eight minutes. Concerned for possible embarrassment to their Chinese hosts, Stern cut four more minutes. Everything else along the way had been smiles, crowds and mutual wonderment. But a badly maintained piano in Shanghai was unplayable, the management insisted that it was the best available, and Stern, nearly in orbit, threatened to call Beijing, if that's what it took, to airlift a substitute. Remarkably, a substitute was found without leaving town. The scene was saved, but carefully smoothed over, and the editors cut from Stern's tantrum to the arrival of the second piano.[50] All that remained was to promote the film and sell it.

It started slowly, Stern remembered. But warm words from Gene Shalit, on the threshold of a forty-year career as resident movie reviewer on *Today*, NBC's signature morning news show, were already down-payment on national attention, Scheuer confirmed in a note of appreciation a decade later.[51] An Academy Award for Best Documentary Feature of 1980 did the rest. Stern's exuberant whoop in Florida, where he had been watching with mild interest, could be heard across the continent, he reported in his memoir.[52]

By November 1981, about a half-year after its release, the film had made it to seven theaters in six states, plus Canada, and was upcoming in fourteen, including the District of Columbia. It even made money for Carnegie Hall. A preliminary budget estimated production costs at $213,989.06. By the end of 1981, it had already grossed $1,205,934. In 1982, it showed in Cannes.

Stern personally dispatched a copy to Charles, Prince of Wales, on the occasion of his marriage to Lady Diana Spencer. "Among the many gifts you will be receiving on this occasion of your wedding one could venture a guess that few would concern themselves with youth, and music, an area for which you have shown great appreciation and affection,"[53] said the note that accompanied it. Scheuer forwarded a couple of cassettes to Kissinger with compliments from Stern as well as himself. By a convenient coincidence, A. M. Rosenthal, executive editor of the *New York Times*, was en route to Beijing. Stern asked him to hand-carry a copy of the film to Huang Hua. Producer to producer, Scheuer sent a VHS cassette to Steven Spielberg. At Stern's suggestion, he also sent a Betamax PAL cassette a few years later to the Queen of Denmark.[54]

Two years after the film's release, a clearly distressed Scheuer informed Kissinger that the authorities in Beijing had not yet released it for general audiences or even conservatory viewing. He hoped a time would come when "kinder hearts and fewer martinets will decide what one billion Chinese will be permitted to enjoy."[55]

But response in the West was both gratifying and interesting. Daniel A. Evans, western regional vice president of the Piano Technicians Guild, wondered about a seminar for Chinese piano technicians. Professor Jean-Philippe Assal of Geneva, a medical educator with a special concern for the treatment of diabetics, pronounced Stern's didactic performance an exemplary transcultural teaching strategy.[56] H. D. Prensky, a Mexico City dentist, reported that a reference to the film with a slide showing Stern in China came in handy in a talk on music and patient management. Tom Robertson of Larkspur, California, was moved to verse.

*Innocent of life and themselves,*
*the children played*
*rigorously, rigidly*
*with grim determination . . .*
*At last he took up the bow*
*and played them a truth*
*words can not say*
*and only art perfected can know.*
*Overcome with astonishment*
*their rapture filled the hall,*
*and East met West*
*in a feast of love.*

By now, his round-number birthdays had become popular celebrations. The sixtieth was occasion for an exemplary portrait of the artist by Stephen Rubin. In successive stages, it reviewed Stern's career from its San Francisco beginnings to Carnegie Hall, to the National Endowment for the Arts and the America-Israel Cultural Foundation, which were milestones of his forties, to the Jerusalem Music Centre, and China, which were milestones of his fifties.[57]

The seventieth was occasion for a benefit concert before an audience of 20,000 in San Francisco's Stern (no relative) Grove. Gregory Peck, who'd known Stern since their National Endowment days, contributed an appreciation. The San Francisco Symphony contributed a performance of Camille Saint-Saëns's *Carnival of the Animals*. Mstislav Rostropovich, in tutu, tights and tiara, appeared as the swan.[58] Yefim Bronfman and Robert

McDonald, two of Stern's favorite pianists, appeared as pianists. Schneider, with violin in one hand, a telephone in the other, and glasses propped up on his forehead, appeared hilariously and unmistakably as Stern.

A perennial challenge, the mail was a daily medley of fan letters, news from old friends, political or charitable solicitations, real estate and market tips, the occasional offer of an academic deanship, requests for recommendations, vocational counseling, autographed photos or advice on the appointment of a conductor or principal violist, appeals for his vote in a ferocious campaign for a new condo board, and recipes for fund-raiser cookbooks.

Occasionally it was improbable, even bizarre. An admirer in Florida wanted him to have a copy of *The Joy of Creating* by L. Ron Hubbard, the creator of Scientology. A sender who identified himself as Jesus Christ of Nazareth wanted him to do something about carbon emissions. An invitation to join the National Republican Advisory Council "because of your proven commitment to the principles and ideals of the Republican Party" found its way into the humor file.

There was also a fifth-grader in Oregon who wanted to know as part of a school assignment in mid-April what Stern's life was like. Where indicated, a couple of tough and competent secretaries were ready with boiler plate. But in this case as in many, he answered in person and in full, although it was late May before he found time to reply. "When the letters are interesting enough, I answer them myself," he explained to an inquirer in Cincinnati.[59] As a rule, he was not one to brush off a curious eleven-year-old.

Worthy of the question, his answer was sensible, informative and unpretentious. "It is filled with rehearsals, concerts, recordings, television and listening to gifted young people in the United States, Israel and in other countries where I do a great deal of work," he told the boy. "I am also interested in the life around us and care very much about the quality of life as it is influenced by the political climate."[60]

Though not quite of comparable gravitas, his response to a query from Emma, another young correspondent, was also interesting. "Do you like being on TV?" she asked. "Sure," he replied. "Who doesn't?" He enjoyed travel too, he added, which was a good thing "in as much [as] I have to travel to play concerts."[61]

He had, by now, reduced his concert schedule to four or five months a year, concentrated increasingly on chamber music with a cadre of younger friends, and went only where he wanted to go. But he was still among the world's most frequent fliers, addressing legislatures, lobbying Congress, and aiming for Jerusalem in alternate summers, where he presided over what were still referred to as master classes, but he preferred to call Encounters. First in Jerusalem at the Music Centre, then Carnegie Hall, Amsterdam, Cologne and Miyazaki, they would be his last major project.

They were not for the faint of heart. Tough love had been an elemental part of his own formative experience since Blinder had invited him to play with his orchestra colleagues. The most professional of the city's pros, they expected a kid who played with the grown-ups to play like a grown-up and hammered him if he didn't.[62]

Dorothy DeLay, a favorite colleague as well as one of the

era's most successful teachers, was a product of small-town, Middle American nice, and a father with a passion for John Dewey, the prophet of learn-by-doing progressive education. "Tell me, sugarplum," she would famously ask a student. "What's your concept of B-flat?" As even his most distinguished protégés could confirm from personal experience, Stern did not do sugarplums.

Joel Smirnoff, a veteran of the Juilliard Quartet, wrote to thank him for hearing one of Smirnoff's students. "And I promise to 'give her hell,' as you have advised," he added.[63] He was tough on everyone, said Miriam Fried, another Stern protégée and a Queen Elisabeth winner. "There were times when I was so angry I never wanted to talk to him again," she remembered.[64] But she also noted and regretted that he had no successor.

In principle, "give 'em hell" could have been the slogan of Stern's Encounters. The target participants were the best and brightest young chamber ensembles, drawn from a pool of demand that far exceeded supply. The rules specified that they be fifteen to thirty, with a bit of entry-level stage experience already under their belts. Seated a few rows in front of them, rather like a general surrounded by senior staff officers, were Stern and a cadre of globally distinguished younger colleagues, whose collective experience could add up to 250 years. A walk-on audience looked on with interest.

It was understood over the next two weeks that they would dissect and examine phrases, even individual measures, with minimal likelihood that any single movement would be heard to the end. "Like going 12 rounds with Mike Tyson," said a young

English violist.[65] "Bambi meets Godzilla," said Philip Setzer of the Emerson Quartet.[66] In Amsterdam, it was reported, one of the participants cried.

"He is aware that a strong reaction from him can change someone's life and is not afraid to use shock treatment if people need it," said David Finckel, a founding member of the Emerson Quartet as well as Setzer's colleague and Stern's regular sideman. Furious with a young quartet that refused to get the message in Cologne, Stern grabbed the violinist James Buswell by the forearm. "Feel my pulse," he said.[67] He then disappeared with the offending quartet and read them the riot act.

But more usual in Setzer's experience was the player who rallied the troops when one or another wanted to retreat. "I know that some students were a bit traumatized," he reported from a session in Jerusalem, "but they all played much better by the end of the sessions."[68] A brave—or badly-briefed—local TV reporter asked Stern whether his sessions made a difference. "That is without a doubt the stupidest question I've ever been asked," Stern replied.

Like the sixtieth and seventieth, his eightieth birthday was an occasion. But this time, it extended over half a year and four concerts. The names in the respective concert programs were unlikely to surprise. From Leon Fleisher, b. 1928, to Sarah Chang, b. 1980, they spanned his career.

There was also a private party in the garden of his country house, where he invited Fay Vincent, the former Commissioner of Baseball and Friend of Isaac from Connecticut, to sit next to him at dinner. "He once told me to think of him as a fat little kid from San Francisco who loved Joe DiMaggio," Vincent reminisced.[69]

In September 2000, the date closest to his actual birthday in July, the official celebration began, again no surprise, with a gala concert in Carnegie Hall's Isaac Stern Auditorium. Ma contributed Saint-Saëns's unsinkable *Swan*, with narration by Sir Peter Ustinov, himself within a year of eighty. Midori and Zukerman contributed the Mozart Sinfonia Concertante for violin and viola. Betty Comden and Adolph Green, Friends of Isaac as well as Carnegie Hall, contributed Bernstein show tunes with lyrics by themselves. An ad hoc ensemble, well stocked with Juilliard and Guarneri Quartet players, and anchored by Jian Wang, the cellist first seen years earlier as an adorable nine-year-old in *From Mao to Mozart*, contributed two movements of the Mendelssohn Octet.

As the finale, Kurt Masur, conductor of the New York Philharmonic, piloted Carnegie staff through Ernst Toch's Geographical Fugue for spoken chorus. An engaging specimen of Weimar Republican rap by yet another member of the Hollywood diaspora, it dated back to 1930. It was now revised for the occasion to accommodate places unmentioned in the original text, but significant in Stern's career. Everyone in the packed house pitched in for "Happy Birthday."[70]

In October, there was a proxy concert in Los Angeles. Stern, recovering in New York from open-heart surgery, addressed the audience by video. In his absence, he was represented by two protégés, the pianist Yefim Bronfman and the violinist Gil Shaham, who flew in as pinch-hit soloists. Conductor Esa-Pekka

Salonen and the orchestra's managing director, Deborah Borda, told funny Stern stories.[71]

The following March there was a third concert, this one at the Kennedy Center in Washington. It was preceded by dinner with much of the Washington Performing Arts Society, Katherine Graham of the *Washington Post* and the ambassadors of Colombia, Germany, Israel and the Netherlands. "He officially turned 80 last July," *Washington Life Magazine* noted, "but turning 80 entitles you to celebrate your birthday all year long, if you choose to, doesn't it?"

With himself in the unfamiliar role of second violinist to Setzer, he then joined three members of the Emerson Quartet and Jonathan Biss, the pianist son of Miriam Fried, in the world premiere of a piano quintet by William Bolcom. There was a follow-up performance in Boston. They were probably his last concerts.

Though reportedly advised against it, he returned to Japan in early May, with plans to come home via Korea, where he was curious to understand where all those terrific young violinists came from. But he already complained of shortness of breath on arrival and felt almost ill enough to cancel his engagement in Miyazaki.[72] As it had for six decades, the show went on as scheduled. But there was no Korea. Instead, he went home to a second open-heart surgery and died eleven days after the attack on the World Trade Center. The cause of death was listed as heart failure.

Twenty-six paid notices in the *New York Times* were already a measure of the galaxy he called home. Among the senders were four orchestras, plus the Metropolitan Opera; the Lincoln and Kennedy Centers as well as Carnegie Hall; Juilliard, Curtis and the

Manhattan School; his lawyer, Bella Linden, the family of Itzhak Perlman, and the Lotos Club. Head-of-state–, Aretha Franklin–level obits appeared within the week, many within a day.

Comprehensive and consensual, they gravitated to the same bullet points. An obit for the Italian magazine *Amadeus* by Maria Majno Golub, the wife of Stern's pianist in China, was a bit of an outlier, but only for a little joke on "well-rounded" and "many-sided," with its implied reference to Stern's physical as well as his intellectual profile.[73] It was a joke Stern might have told on himself. The draft also recalled the scene in China where Stern, who hated patent shoulder rests with a passion, delighted his audience by producing his "secret," a foam rubber cushion, from under his shirt.

But everyone agreed that he'd been a great player and exemplary citizen, whose playing had declined as his civic activity increased; that he'd advanced the cause of chamber music like none of his contemporaries; saved Carnegie Hall; built bridges to Israel and China; demonstratively played and introduced living composers; devoted himself with skill and passion, if admittedly mixed success, to the cause of music education; and caused the sun to shine on the next generation of young talents. It was also tactfully but unmistakably acknowledged that there were some who felt they had been unfairly and undeservedly left in the shade.[74]

Adolph Green, literally as well as figuratively a close neighbor at the Beresford, recalled a man who stood by wounded Israeli soldiers and frightened civilians in moments of existential threat; shared a New Year's Eve with his neighbors by making his way through the Mozart sonatas with his friend Lenny, and played tennis like "a nimble and very aggressive bowling ball." There was a fond reminiscence of Stern's funeral, where Istomin unloaded affectionately on his longtime partner. "OK, Isaac, now the truth has to come out," he said. "You made a lousy martini."[75]

On October 30, people were lined up around the block at 10 A.M. for 800 free tickets to a memorial concert at 3 P.M. in what had been the Stern Auditorium since 1997. Four hundred more listeners followed the concert on closed-circuit TV in other rooms. Rather than call on the audience to stand for the usual moment of silence, Sanford Weill, Carnegie Hall's current chairman, invited it to stand and applaud. The rest was music.

A representative ensemble of veterans played movements of Beethoven, Mozart, Dvořák and Brahms that they had also played with Stern. A pair of representative juniors, participants in Stern's final Encounters, were co-opted for a movement of the Brahms sextet, Op. 18. Everyone went home with a Sony CD of the Mozart piano quartets Stern had recorded with Ma, Laredo and Emanuel Ax.[76]

His legacy was as many-sided as the man himself. The program alone listed forty-four honors of one sort or another dating back to 1956. Among them were fourteen honorary degrees from three countries, medals from six and twelve more foreign awards. The Israel Philharmonic, the St. Louis Symphony and the Philharmonic Society of New York had all declared him an honorary member. The San Francisco Symphony endowed a first violin chair in his name.

But there was more. In February 1981, Martin S. Brown,

president of the Jack Daniel Distillery, was delighted to inform him that he had been elected to the Tennessee Squire Association, "formed many years ago to acknowledge those friends of our distillery and of our Tennessee whiskey." As "an admirer of the sender's 'noble liquid,' " Stern replied immediately and in person that he was delighted, honored and looked forward to a site visit.[77]

In October of the same year, Cyril Clemens, editor of the *Mark Twain Journal*, informed him that he had been voted the Mark Twain Gold Medal "in recognition of your contribution to modern music." Stern's secretary replied that he had just left for the airport but expressed his thanks in absentia.[78]

In 1992, he showed *Small Wonders*, his friend Wally Scheuer's film on Roberta Guaspari, to fellow members of the Lotos Club. He even brought Guaspari in person as a dinner guest, as well as Arnold Steinhardt of the Guarneri Quartet to play for no more than ten minutes between the second course and dessert.

In 1994, Edward C. Carter II congratulated Stern on his election to the American Philosophical Society, created by Benjamin Franklin in 1743. As its distinguished and energetic librarian,[79] Carter hoped that Stern, like many members, might also become a Friend of the Library.[80] Stern at least volunteered a paper: "Quality of Life." But he unfortunately had to cancel when reminded by the tireless Lamont that the scheduled presentation conflicted with rehearsals in Baltimore and concerts already scheduled in Japan.[81]

In death as in life, the list went on. On October 9, 2001, Will Shortz, the puzzle editor of the *New York Times*, wrote him into a crossword puzzle as "late great violinist" at 61-across.[82] Miyazaki named a concert hall with 1,997 seats for him. Tel Aviv named a street.

In 2016, Shanghai carried his legacy a great leap further with the inauguration of an international violin competition in his name. A creation of the violinist Vera Tsu Weiling, the conductor Long Yu and the Shanghai Symphony in a joint venture with Stern's sons, the competition was as much epigraph as a geopolitical metaphor. For all four sponsors, Stern's visit in 1979 had been as seminal for themselves as Kissinger's had been for China's place in the world seven years before.

In 1920, the year Stern was born, the past, present and presumably future of the violin were represented by little Jewish boys, and aspiring artists looked to Europe. In 1935, violinists everywhere looked to Warsaw, and a pioneer competition in memory of the great Henryk Wieniawski. In 1937, all roads led to Brussels and the Queen Elisabeth Competition, created as a memorial to the great Eugène Ysaÿe. Little more than a generation later, Pinchas Zukerman of Israel and Kyung Wha Chung of Korea aimed for the Leventritt Competition in New York. In 1982, Joseph Gingold, a familiar and respected judge at other people's competitions in Brussels and Moscow, became the namesake and dedicatee of his own competition in Indianapolis.

But that was the twentieth century. It was now the twenty-first, and the venue alone was a geocultural statement. Years before, David Stern noted in an interview with violinist and journalist Laurie Niles,[83] Paris had dropped competitions honoring the great cellist Rostropovich and the great flautist Jean-Pierre

Rampal because it could no longer afford them. Generously underwritten by the city of Shanghai under a long-term contract, first, second and third prizes of $100,000, $50,000 and $25,000 respectively exceeded anything to date. There was even an Isaac Stern Human Spirit Award, bestowed in 2016 on Negin Khpalwak, the creator of Afghanistan's first all-female orchestra.

A balanced aquarium of a jury, made up respectively of soloists, chamber players, concertmasters, teachers and managers, was another novelty, and judges' names and scores, all posted online, were unique in the history of the institution. The hoops and hurdles expected of the contestants were new too. Among them were a concerto, a solo sonata, a string quartet, a new cadenza of the contestant's composition, and a piece by Qigang Chen, a survivor of the Cultural Revolution, who had settled in France and studied with Olivier Messiaen. A kind of Olympic pentathlon, they reflected Stern's idea of the essence and future of the profession.

Like Stern, his friend Felix Rohatyn was an immigrant who made good. At forty-seven, he saved New York from bankruptcy as Stern saved Carnegie Hall from the wreckers. At sixty-nine, he was appointed ambassador to France. Rohatyn was so intelligent that even the French would want to listen to him, Stern told Sylvie Kauffmann of *Le Monde*. He dismissed the idea that the ambassadorship would be Rohatyn's grand finale. His career would continue till his last day, Stern assured her. "His life is his career."[84]

With lives in the plural, the same could be said of Isaac Stern. Name, dates, vocation or, better still, persona, it was all spelled out with exquisite concision and a hint of self-irony on the headstone in the suburban Connecticut cemetery where he was buried.

ISAAC STERN

JULY 21, 1920

SEPTEMBER 22, 2001

FIDDLER

The traditional pebbles that visitors left on the headstone bore witness to a Jewish grave. Acquired respectively by the Nippon Foundation and BSI of Lugano, Switzerland, his del Gesùs carried on his legacy under new management.

# Notes

## Preface

1. Robert Bein to author, July 17, 2004.
2. David Schoenbaum, *The Violin: A Social History of the World's Most Versatile Instrument* (New York, 2012).
3. Norman Lebrecht to author, September 12, 2017.

## I. Immigrant

1. Boulanger to Stern, September 21, 1953; Orchestra Committee to Vera Lindenblit Stern, January 18, 1954.
2. Stern to R. Philip Hanes, August 17, 1994; Hanes to Stern, September 20, 1994.
3. William F. Buckley, *Happy Days Were Here Again* (New York, 1993), p. 337.
4. Robert H. Bork, "Ambrosia and Amnesia," *National Review*, November 25, 1996; Stern, Reader's Letter, *National Review*, December 11, 1996.
5. Undated note attached to letter addressed to Mary Lou Falcone, April 4, 1990.
6. Isaac Stern, *My First 79 Years* (New York, 1999), p. 156.
7. Noah Stern Weber to author, September 26, 2017.

8. Stern to Cooke, March 27, 1973.
9. Stern, *My First 79 Years*, p. 52.
10. *New York Times*, November 30, 1986.
11. Milton Gordon to Stern, January 31, 1994.
12. Harry E. Milchen to Jacques Francais, December 29, 1971, Stern Papers, Library of Congress.

## II. Professional

1. C. F. Flesch to Stern, July 14, 1972, Stern to C. F. Flesch, August 8, 1972.
2. Arnold Steinhardt, http://keyofstrawberry.com/luggage/, December 4, 2017.
3. Stern, *My First 79 Years*, p. 109.
4. Karen Shaffer and Neva Greenwood, *Maud Powell* (Arlington, VA, and Ames, IA, 1988), p. 277.
5. Myriam Anissimov, "Une Mafia du Violon?" *Le Monde de la Musique*, May 1984.
6. Joseph Wechsberg, "The Long Phrase," *New Yorker*, June 5, 1965.
7. Joseph Horowitz, *Classical Music in America* (New York, 2007), p. 197.
8. *Washington Post*, November 15, 1939.
9. Horowitz, *Classical Music in America*, pp. 395ff.
10. Roland Gelatt, "Isaac Stern: The Rise of an American Virtuoso," *High Fidelity*, May 1956.
11. Interview with Martin Goldsmith, *Book TV*, C-Span2, December 14, 1999.
12. Purves v. ICM Artists, Ltd., 119 B.R. 407 (S.D.N.Y. 1990).
13. Barbara Jepson, "Managing Musical Superstars," *New York Times*, September 24, 1989; Matthew Gurewitsch, "Presenting Lee Lamont," *Manhattan, inc.*, February 1986.

14. "Isaac Stern Gives Unusual Recital," *New York Times*, December 10, 1945.
15. "Recital: Stern with McDonald, at Carnegie Hall," *New York Times*, May 6, 1987.
16. "Isaac Stern, Violinist, Heard in Carnegie Hall," *New York Herald Tribune*, January 9, 1943.
17. "Heifetz Aids Vassar Club" and "Isaac Stern Gives 4th Recital Here," *New York Times*, January 9, 1943.
18. Quoted in Stern, *My First 79 Years*, pp. 38–39.
19. Jean Spencer Felton to Stern, November 3, 2000.
20. Obituary, *Journal of Occupational and Environmental Medicine*, August 2003, p. 779.
21. Roland Gelatt, "The Rise of an American Virtuoso," *Hi-Fi*, May 1956.
22. Stern, *My First 79 Years*, p. 110.
23. Harold C. Schonberg, "Soaring Fees for Star Musicians Are Disrupting the Concert World," *New York Times*, November 30, 1980.
24. John Kongsgaard interview with the author, December 30, 2016.
25. Harold C. Schonberg, "Isaac Stern Is Too Busy to Retire," *New York Times*, December 4, 1984.
26. Sol Hurok to Serge Koussevitzky, January 17, 1946.
27. Maxim Gershunoff and Leon Van Dyke, *It's Not All Song and Dance* (Pompton Plains, NJ, 2005), pp. 45–46.
28. Bosley Crowther, "The Screen in Review," *New York Times*, December 26, 1946; "Top Grossers of 1947," *Variety*, January 7, 1948.
29. Susan Koppelman to Stern, January 6, 1987; Naomi Steinberger to Susan Koppelman, January 27, 1987.
30. Stern to Karl Thorson, May 10, 2000.
31. Viz. Lon Tuck, "Isaac Stern," *Washington Post*, October 5, 1980; Foreign Assets Control, Foreign Relations Department, Federal Reserve Bank of New York to Stern, May 21, 1982.
32. Harold A. Keiser to Stern, July 29, 1997.

33. Teddy Kollek to Mrs. Vera Stern, February 24, 1991.
34. Robert Coggeshall to Caroline Saccucci, June 15, 2017, made available to the author.
35. Stern, *My First 79 Years*, p. 33.
36. Stern to Lutie Goldstein, December 27, 1952; Stern to Walter Prude, October 4, 1953; Stern to "Maisele," October 10, 1953, Stern to Martin Feinstein, November 7, 1953.
37. Victor Paranjoti to Stern, October 28, 1953.
38. Robert Commanday, Music, *San Francisco Chronicle*, July 27, 1980.
39. Stern, *My First 79 Years*, pp. 107–8; Maya Magub to author, January 27, 2017; K. F. Sanjana to Stern, October 19, 1953; Victor Paranjoti to Stern, October 28, 1953; Stern to Sanjana, November 8, 1953.
40. Stern, *My first 79 Years*, p. 190.
41. Stern, *My first 79 Years*, p. 88; Alexander Schneider, *Sasha: A Musician's Life* (self-published, c. 1987), pp. 114ff. and 134.
42. Casals to Stern, December 20, 1952; Jean-Pierre Molkhou, "Pour l'Amour de la Musique," *Diapason*, August 1995.
43. Hiroko Tobari, Casals Hall, to Stern, July 9, 1987; Stern to Hiroko Tobari, August 3, 1987; Lynne Normandia to Ira Rosenblum, March 30, 2000.
44. James Wade, "Vast Symphony Gets 1st Performance," *Korea Times*, September 23, 1971.
45. Stern, *My First 79 Years*, p. 169.
46. Schneider to Stern, undated.
47. Robert Jacobson, "The Intellectual, the Gambler, and the Corporate Man," *High Fidelity*, May 1972, p. 55.
48. Viz. James Gollin, *Pianist* (Bloomington, IN, 2010), pp. 250ff.
49. Jacobson, "The Intellectual."
50. Stern to Markevitch, July 29, 1953.
51. Stern to Balint Andras Varga, September 27, 1978.
52. Stern to Mrs. Hindemith, May 1, 1964.
53. Stern, *My First 79 Years*, p. 237.
54. Ormandy to Stern, September 4, 1967.

55. William N. Tuttle to Stern, June 22, 1983; Stern to William N. Tuttle, March 1, 1985.
56. Joseph W. Polisi, "The William Schuman Violin Concerto," Project Muse, Notes, March 2010.
57. Bernstein to Stern, July 12, September 12, and October 8, 1954; Stern to Bernstein, June 24, 1955.
58. "George Rochberg, Composer, Dies at 86," *New York Times*, June 1, 2005.
59. Bob Holton, Belwin-Mills Publishing Corp., to Stern, August 22, 1973; Stern to Penderecki, June 15, 1977.
60. Stern to Lee Lamont, June 22, 1987.
61. Stern, *My First 79 Years*, pp. 274–75; Stern to Hanne Wilhelm Hansen, December 23, 1985; Bruce Duffie interview with Isaac Stern, Chicago, May 27, 1991.
62. Donal Henahan, "Stern Plays Maxwell Davies Concerto," *New York Times*, May 14, 1988.
63. Isaac Stern, New York, April 11, 1993.
64. Isaac Stern, *My First 79 Years*, p. 275.
65. Stern to Rossier, January 17 and April 10, 1968; Rossier to "Dear Friends," February 6, 1968.
66. Paul Wheeler to Stern, May 14, 1968; Stern to Mrs. Olga Jovanović, October 10, 1969.
67. Curt Schleier, "Isaac Stern Lifts the Spirit with His Passion for Music," *Milwaukee Journal-Sentinel*, October 13, 1999.

## III. Public Citizen

1. Ward Halstead to Stern, March 1, 1950.
2. Stern, *My First 79 Years*, p. 41.
3. Mike Vogel, "He and Violin Great Shared Tent," *Buffalo Evening News*, January 14, 1980.
4. George Manolakes to Stern, December 16, 1986.

5. Carl Mattes to Stern, undated.
6. Stern, *My First 79 Years*, p. 44.
7. Terry Klefstad, "Shostakovich and the Peace Conference," *Music & Politics* 6, no. 2 (Summer 2012); Philip Deery, "Shostakovich, the Waldorf Conference and the Cold War," *American Communist History* 11, no. 2 (2012).
8. Stern to Cedric Belfrage, November 19, 1968.
9. Isaac Stern, "Cultural Mission in Iceland," *New York Times*, January 23, 1955.
10. John J. Muccio to Stern, January 28, 1955; G. Hayden Raynor to Stern, January 31, 1955.
11. Letter to Martin, possibly Bookspan, November 7, 1953.
12. "Un Américain a Moscou," *Le Figaro*, January 30, 1956.
13. Umberto Masini and Michele Selvini, "Isaac Stern," *Musica*, March 1985.
14. Statement regarding Oistrakh for CBS Homage Record Insert, undated 1974.
15. Stern, *My First 79 Years*, p. 119.
16. B. J. Cutler, "Soviets Won't Submit to U.S. Fingerprinting," *New York Herald Tribune*, June 1, 1956; Stern to Bohlen, June 5, 1956; Bohlen to Stern, July 3, 1956.
17. Harlow Robinson, *Impresario* (New York, 1994), p. 350; James Loeffler, "How an American Opera Star Accidentally Launched the Soviet Jewish Movement," *Tablet*, June 30, 2016.
18. P. Yeshov to Stern, May 27, 1960.
19. Stern to Walter Prude, August 23, 1968, Stern, *My First 79 Years*, p. 203.
20. Dimitri Drobatschewsky, "Isaac Stern's Love of Music, Life Remains Undiminished," *Arizona Republic*, February 5, 1988.
21. Letter from Amsterdam, no addressee indicated, October 11, 1949.
22. *Chicago Sun-Times*, August 19, 1993.
23. Stern to Lady Dorothy de Rothschild, February 27, 1986.
24. Gluzman interview with the author, June 3, 2017; Stern to Defense

Minister Yitzhak Rabin, undated draft, 1984; Stern to Minister of Education and Culture Zevulun Hammer, June 12, 1984.

25. Interview with Martin Bookspan, January 13, 1971; William E. Wiener Oral History Library of the American Jewish Committee, New York Public Library.
26. Proposed project for Jerusalem, Israel, December 1972 and January 1973, May 7, 1971.
27. Sally Wells to Ruth Leon et al., August 3, 1977.
28. Stern, *My First 79 Years*, pp. 242–43.
29. Stern, *My First 79 Years*, p. 159.
30. Stern, *My First 79 Years*, p. 143ff.
31. Stern interview, New York, Preservation Project, J. M. Kaplan Fund; Wolfgang Saxon, "Jacob Kaplan, Philanthropist, Is Dead," *New York Times*, July 20, 1987.
32. Richard S. Childs, "Carnegie Hall Opposed," March 28, 1960, p. 28.
33. Stern, *My First 79 Years*, p. 147.
34. "Talk of the Town," *New Yorker*, April 9, 1960, pp. 30–31.
35. Stern to Rubinstein, June 9, 1960.
36. Dedication of Carnegie Hall, WNYC, New York Public Radio, November 6, 1964.
37. Public Broadcasting Service, "A Time to Remember," first shown on PBS, November 21, 1988.
38. "WPA Maestro," *Time*, March 29, 1939, p. 54.
39. John F. Kennedy, "The Arts in America," *Look*, December 18, 1962.
40. Interview with Brian Lamb, "Booknotes," C-Span, January 30, 2000; Stern, *My First 79 Years*, pp. 268–69.
41. Charles Christopher Mark, *Reluctant Bureaucrats* (Dubuque, IA, 1990), pp. 118–21.
42. Ari L. Goldman, "Musicians in Philharmonic Boycott Harlem Church," *New York Times*, December 19, 1986.
43. James C. Stratton, "Arts Festival," *Stillwater (OK) News-Press*, November 1, 1964.
44. Stern to the Hon. Mario M. Cuomo, March 29, 1989.

45. State Sen. Richard J. Cohen to Stern, June 17, 1995.
46. Susan Edelman, "Crew Urging City Leaders to Found Charter Schools," *New York Post*, February 2, 1999.
47. Abby Goodnough, "43 School Superintendents Do Their Best Jack Benny," *New York Times*, May 11, 2000.

## IV. Chairman of the Board

1. Jacques Barzun, *God's Country and Mine* (Boston, 1954).
2. Henry Luce, "The American Century," *Life*, February 17, 1941.
3. Shalom Goldman, "Mr. Sinatra Adored Israel," *Tablet*, May 14, 2015.
4. Shawn Amos, "Why Frank Sinatra Is Still the Chairman After 100 Years," https://sinatrafamily.com/forum/showthread.php/48353.
5. Jeff Giles, "To Play and Play Again: How Frank Sinatra's Thirst for Creative Freedom Led to Some of Classic Rock's Greatest Records," *Ultimate Classic Rock*, undated.
6. Lawrence P. Goldman, director of real estate development and planning, to Mayor Ed. Koch; Amy Pagnozzi, "Sinatra Does It His Way to Raise 250G," *New York Post*, June 5, 2016.
7. Allan Kozinn, "Holiday for Strings," *New York Times*, December 24, 1998.
8. "A Program for Carnegie Hall, A Feasibility Study," September 1982, unpublished.
9. Paula Span, "Carnegie's Comeback," *Washington Post*, December 16, 1986.
10. Stern, *My First 79 Years*, p. 193
11. Stern-Potok draft transcript.
12. John Rockwell, "Carnegie, Renewed at 95, Is Again the Premiere Hall," and Anne-Marie Schiro, "A Marathon of Parties for Carnegie Hall," *New York Times*, December 16, 1986.
13. Lynne Normandia to Pat Krol, September 9, 1998.

14. Stern, *My First 79 Years*, pp. 285–86.
15. Leslie Bennetts, "How Carnegie Hall Has Evolved into a 'Business,' " *New York Times*, May 31, 1983.
16. Earl Wild, *A Walk on the Wild Side* (Palm Springs, CA, 2011), pp. 472–84.
17. Lawrence P. Goldman to Stern, September 17, 1987.
18. Andrew Porter, "Musical Events," *New Yorker*, August 1, 1988; Robert A. Kadison to Stern, October 5, 1988.
19. Peter Kroll to Stern, September 9, 1988; Stern to Peter Kroll, October 3, 1988.
20. Allan Kozinn to author, June 17, 2017.
21. Jay Golan to Stern, Re: "Belongingness," October 4, 1993.
22. Susan Shine to Stern, March 22, 30, 1993.
23. Itzhak Perlman to "Dear Isaac and Vera," September 10, 1985.
24. Lois Applebaum Leibow, *The Strad*, April 1976, p. 895.
25. Frederick Gash to Arthur Doty, April 6, 1977.
26. Ram Evron to Stern, February 16, 1992, Stern inquiry, Jerusalem Music Centre, October 6, 1993.
27. Stern to Board, July 22, 1975.
28. Ruth Leon to Theodore Conant, November 21, 1980.
29. Ruth Leon to author, September 11, 2017.
30. Kollek to Irwin S. Field, Santa Fe Springs, CA, January 2, 1980.
31. Clyde Haberman, "A Flood of Soviet Immigrants Brings a Glut of Musicians to Israel," *New York Times*, April 7, 1992.
32. Fried to Stern, February 20, 1986.
33. Stern to Dorothy de Rothschild, February 27, 1986.
34. Gluzman interview with the author, June 3, 2017.
35. Peled interview with the author, September 5, 2017.
36. Ivan Stefanovic to author, September 27, 2016.
37. *Baltimore Sun*, November 22, 1997.
38. Bernard Holland, "Five Young People Display Their Talents," *New York Times*, January 2, 1983.

39. Stern, *My First 79 Years*, p. 265.
40. Stern to Akio Morita, April 7, 1983.
41. Shmuel Tatz to Stern, February 17, 1993.
42. Midori, *Einfach Midori* (Berlin, 2004), pp. 193–94.
43. Stern, *My First 79 Years*, pp. 163–65; Steven Honigberg, *Leonard Rose* (Silver Spring, MD), p. 283.
44. Yo-Yo Ma, "Isaac Stern, the Artist as Enabler," *New York Times*, October 14, 1990.
45. Arièle Butaux, "Shlomo Mintz et Ses Amis," *Le Monde de la Musique*, August 1990.
46. Joseph Horowitz, *Classical Music in America* (New York, 2007), p. 491.
47. Laurie Niles, "From Mao to Mozart to Now," *Violinist.com*, September 15, 2016.
48. Scheuer to Dr. Richard Collins, April 29, 1991.
49. Jeffrey Scheuer, "Introduction," https://www.jscheuer.com/nl-son-introductionfilm-festival.
50. Stern, *My First 79 Years*, pp. 253–54; Richard F. Shepard, "Isaac Stern in China," *New York Times*, February 23, 1981.
51. Scheuer to Gene Shalit, August 3, 1990.
52. Stern, *My First 79 Years*, p. 254.
53. Stern to HRH The Prince of Wales, July 10, 1981.
54. Scheuer to HM The Queen of Denmark, March 12, 1985.
55. Scheuer to Kissinger, August 5, 1983.
56. Jean-Philippe Assal to Lamont, July 13, 1987.
57. Stephen E. Rubin, "The Power and the Glory," *New York Times*, October 14, 1979.
58. "Celebrating Isaac Stern's 70th Birthday in 1990," *SFGate*, June 3, 2012.
59. Stern to Brian D. Seltzer, January 4, 1994.
60. Stern to Joel Smith, May 27, 1992.
61. Reply to Emma, otherwise unidentified, no date.
62. Stern, *My First 79 Years*, pp. 19–20.

63. Smirnoff to Stern, January 18, 1997.
64. Interview with the author, June 14, 2017.
65. David Schoenbaum, "A Violinist, Passing the Torch, Closes a Circle," *New York Times*, May 23, 1999.
66. Philip Setzer, "A Passion to Teach," *New York Times*, September 17, 2000.
67. Interview with the author, June 14, 2017.
68. Setzer to the author, January 10, 2018.
69. Francis T. (Fay) Vincent Jr., "Between the Notes," *America*, November 5, 2001.
70. Bernard Holland, "A Parade of Youth and Stars for Stern," *New York Times*, September 26, 2000.
71. Mark Swed, "80 Candles," *Los Angeles Times*, October 7, 2000.
72. Carl Samit to Lynne Normandia, May 3, 2001.
73. Maria Majno, "La Stella di Stern," *Amadeus*, February 2002.
74. Viz. Allan Kozinn, "Violinist Isaac Stern Dies at 81," *New York Times*, September 23, 2001; K. Robert Schwarz, "Isaac Stern," *The Guardian*, September 23, 2001; "Isaac Stern," *The Times* (London), September 24, 2001; "Isaac Stern 1920–2001," *International Musician*, November 2001; Maria Majno, "La Stella di Stern."
75. Adolph Green, "My Neighbour Isaac," *The Strad*, April 2002.
76. Anthony Tommasini, "Isaac Stern Recalled at His Carnegie Hall," *New York Times*, October 31, 2001.
77. Martin S. Brown to Stern, February 6, 1981; Stern to Martin S. Brown, March 16, 1981.
78. Cyril Clemens to Stern, October 12, 1981.
79. Mary Maples Dunn, Richard S. Dunn, John C. Van Horne, "Edward C. Carter, II," *Proceedings of the American Philosophical Society* 150, no. 1 (March 2006).
80. Carter to Stern, June 23, 1994.
81. Lamont to Jacques Boubli, April 22, 1997.

82. *New York Times*, October 9, 2001; Will Shortz to author, December 26, 2016.
83. *Violinist.com*, September 15, 2016.
84. Sylvie Kauffmann, “De la Finance à la Diplomatie,” *Le Monde*, September 13, 1997.

# Index